THE VICKSBURG CAMPAIGN, 1863

THE VICKSBURG CAMPAIGN, 1863

Grant's Failed Offensives

Chris Mackowski

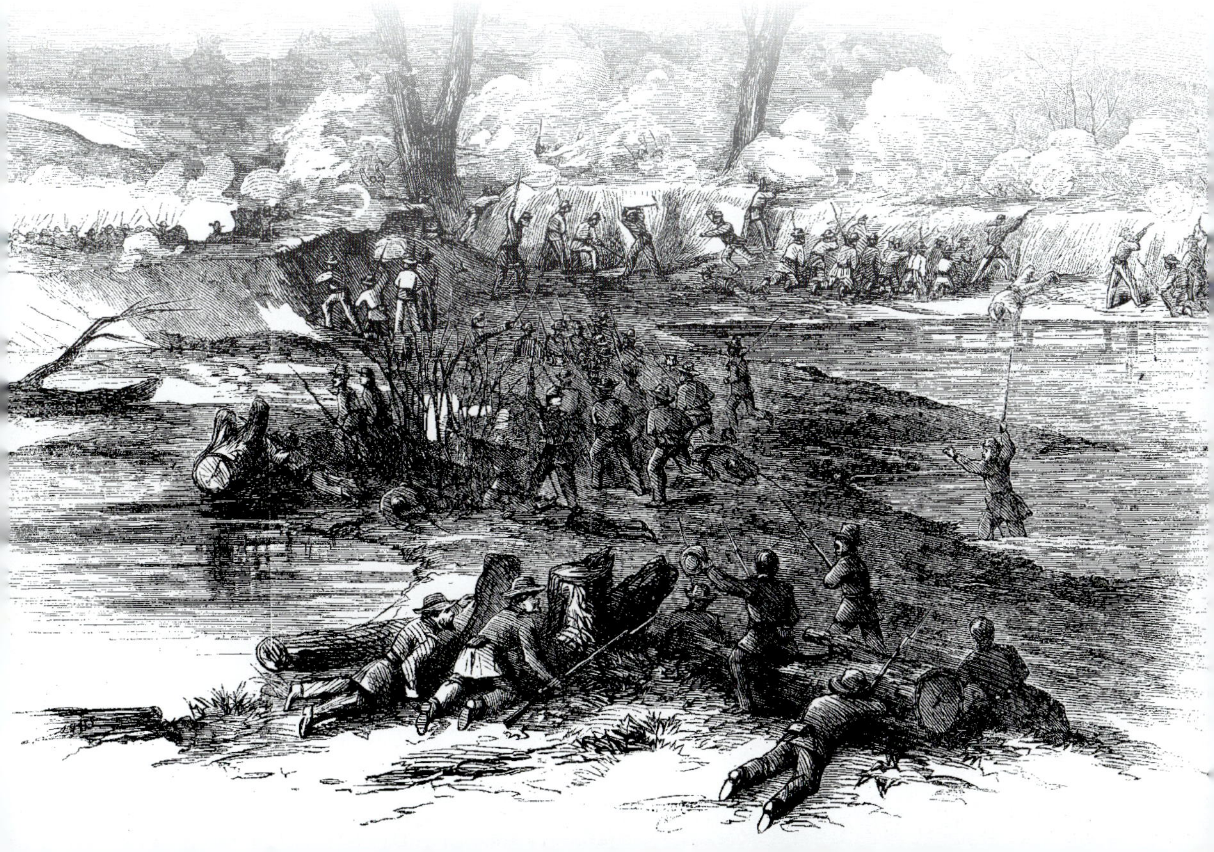

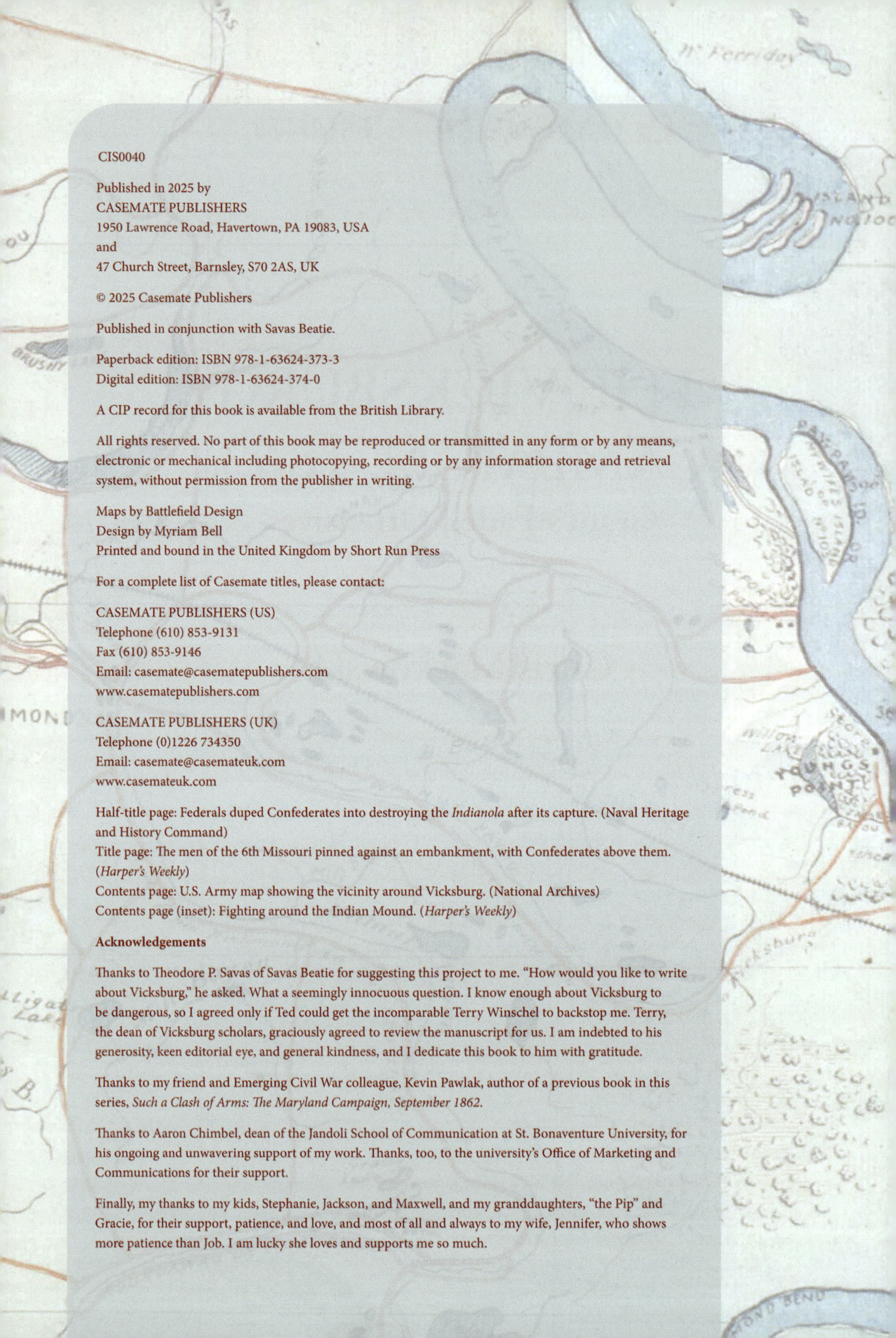

CIS0040

Published in 2025 by
CASEMATE PUBLISHERS
1950 Lawrence Road, Havertown, PA 19083, USA
and
47 Church Street, Barnsley, S70 2AS, UK

Published in conjunction with Savas Beatie.

Paperback edition: ISBN 978-1-63624-373-3
Digital edition: ISBN 978-1-63624-374-0

A CIP record for this book is available from the British Library.

Maps by Battlefield Design
Design by Myriam Bell
Printed and bound in the United Kingdom by Short Run Press

For a complete list of Casemate titles, please contact:

CASEMATE PUBLISHERS (US)
Telephone (610) 853-9131
Fax (610) 853-9146
Email: casemate@casematepublishers.com
www.casematepublishers.com

CASEMATE PUBLISHERS (UK)
Telephone (0)1226 734350
Email: casemate@casemateuk.com
www.casemateuk.com

Half-title page: Federals duped Confederates into destroying the *Indianola* after its capture. (Naval Heritage and History Command)
Title page: The men of the 6th Missouri pinned against an embankment, with Confederates above them. (*Harper's Weekly*)
Contents page: U.S. Army map showing the vicinity around Vicksburg. (National Archives)
Contents page (inset): Fighting around the Indian Mound. (*Harper's Weekly*)

Acknowledgements

Thanks to Theodore P. Savas of Savas Beatie for suggesting this project to me. "How would you like to write about Vicksburg," he asked. What a seemingly innocuous question. I know enough about Vicksburg to be dangerous, so I agreed only if Ted could get the incomparable Terry Winschel to backstop me. Terry, the dean of Vicksburg scholars, graciously agreed to review the manuscript for us. I am indebted to his generosity, keen editorial eye, and general kindness, and I dedicate this book to him with gratitude.

Thanks to my friend and Emerging Civil War colleague, Kevin Pawlak, author of a previous book in this series, *Such a Clash of Arms: The Maryland Campaign, September 1862.*

Thanks to Aaron Chimbel, dean of the Jandoli School of Communication at St. Bonaventure University, for his ongoing and unwavering support of my work. Thanks, too, to the university's Office of Marketing and Communications for their support.

Finally, my thanks to my kids, Stephanie, Jackson, and Maxwell, and my granddaughters, "the Pip" and Gracie, for their support, patience, and love, and most of all and always to my wife, Jennifer, who shows more patience than Job. I am lucky she loves and supports me so much.

BAYOU
YAZOO RIVER
MISSISSIPPI RIVER
RECENTLY CLEARED
DE SOTO
BIG BAYOU
WARRENTON

Contents

Timeline

The Vicksburg Campaign (December 1862–July 1863) consisted of a series of offensive efforts to reach and capture the Confederate river bastion, open the Mississippi River, and completely sever the Confederacy in two. After initial attempts by the U.S. Navy, General Ulysses S. Grant assumed command of the operation in November 1862, although he maintained a strong relationship with his naval counterparts. Grant's first serious attempt was in late 1862 with a direct effort south through Mississippi. The difficult terrain and Confederate defensive measures ended this early thrust. A simultaneous assault under Major General William T. Sherman at Chickasaw Bayou ended in bloody failure. Thereafter, Grant attempted a wide variety of expeditions and complex engineering operations to bypass Vicksburg's heavy gun batteries, none of which was successful. Everything changed in mid-April 1863, when Union vessels discovered they could move downriver past Vicksburg's guns without serious losses. Grant changed his plans by marching his army south down the opposite Louisiana shoreline and crossing the river into the state of Mississippi on April 30, determined to take the city from the south and east.

1862	
May–July	Farragut makes first attempts to capture Vicksburg.
July 23	Henry Halleck promoted to General in Chief of U.S. Army.
October 25	Grant placed in command of the Department of the Tennessee.
November 28	Grant establishes supply base at Holly Springs, Mississippi; sets sights on Oxford, Mississippi.
December 19	Forrest raids Federal supply base in Jackson, Tennessee.
December 20	Van Dorn raids Grant's base at Holly Springs.
December 21	Grant withdraws from Oxford, Mississippi.
December 26–29	Battle of Chickasaw Bayou.

1863 January 9–11	Battle of Arkansas Post.
January 18	Grant takes field command.
January 21	Work begins on the DeSoto Canal.
January 31	Survey works begins on Lake Providence bypass.
February 2	Work begins on clearing Yazoo Pass.
February 23	Work begins on clearing Lake Providence bypass.
February 24	Federal fleet enters Yazoo Pass.
February 24	USS *Indianola* captured.
March 11	First attack on Fort Pemberton.
March 15	Porter begins Steele's Bayou expedition.
March 22	Sherman rescues Porter's gunboats in Steele's Bayou.
March 27	Grant suspends work on the DeSoto Canal.
March 31	Grant's XIII Corps begins march south toward New Carthage.
March 31	Work begins on Duckport Canal.
April 4	Yazoo Pass expedition calls off operations in front of Fort Pemberton.
April 16	Porter runs past the Vicksburg batteries.
April 18	Grant establishes base at Hard Times Landing.
April 22	Army transports run past the Vicksburg batteries.
April 29	Battle of Grand Gulf.
April 30	Grant's army crosses the Mississippi River to begin its inland campaign against Vicksburg.

Introduction

Born along the banks of the Ohio River in 1822, perhaps it's no wonder that Ulysses S. Grant came to know rivers so well. Since the outbreak of the Civil War, he had used the major rivers of the trans-Appalachia as highways into the upper reaches of the Confederate West.

Grant started with headquarters at Cairo, Illinois, at the confluence of the mighty Ohio and Mississippi rivers. In September 1861, he secured Paducah, Kentucky, where the Tennessee River flowed into the Ohio, ensuring access to the interior of Kentucky and, eventually, Tennessee. In November 1861, Grant used the Mississippi to strike south at a Confederate outpost in Belmont, Missouri, earning him and his men their first taste of combat. In February 1862, he used the Tennessee River to strike at Fort Henry. The river ended up doing the work for him, flooding out the fort and forcing its surrender to the U.S. Navy after a brief bombardment. The outcome satisfied the quiet but aggressive Grant, who immediately marched 12 miles east to Fort Donelson on the Cumberland River, where after sharp combat he forced the fort's unconditional surrender a few days later. That, in turn, opened a direct route to Nashville and left the rivers open for gunboats to penetrate deep into its rear. It would be the first Confederate state capital to fall.

▼ Fort Donelson overlooks the Cumberland River. Had the Navy succeeded in forcing the fort's surrender before Grant's infantry arrived, would there have ever been an "Unconditional Surrender" Grant? (Chris Mackowski)

Profile:
Ulysses S. Grant (1822–85)

▲ Grant and his wife Julia had four children: Fred, Ulysses Jr. ("Buck"), Ellen ("Nellie"), and Jesse. He died on July 23, 1885, and is buried in New York City at General Grant National Memorial. (Library of Congress)

Ulysses S. Grant wasn't sure he'd "make the war."

Born in Point Pleasant, Ohio, Grant was a member of the West Point Class of 1843 and a hero of America's war with Mexico. He had left the United States Army in 1854 under a cloud of controversy that continues to dog him into the 21st century. For seven years, he shifted from one struggling endeavor to another, including stints as a farmer and firewood peddler. When civil war broke out in 1861, he had neither the connections or career to ensure a spot in the new volunteer army.

But combat experience was at a premium, and in June, he was appointed colonel of the 21st Illinois. In August, he was promoted to brigadier general.

Grant saw his first combat that November in a small engagement at Belmont, Missouri—a tactical loss but strategic win. In February 1862, he helped develop the plan that led to the capture of Fort Henry on the Tennessee River, and then days later captured Fort Donelson on the Cumberland River, leading to the surrender of Tennessee's capital, Nashville. Those victories led to the first of several conflicts with his immediate supervisor, Major General Henry Halleck, although Grant did not realize Halleck's animosity at the time.

In early April 1862, Grant's army won the battle of Shiloh, the largest and costliest battle that had ever fought in American history up to that point. In the wake of the fight, Grant's troubles with Halleck continued. Halleck was eventually promoted and transferred to Washington, D.C., leaving Grant in command of the department. He won additional victories at Iuka and Corinth, and then set his sights on a campaign to open the Mississippi River.

"The art of war is simple enough," Grant once told a colleague: "find out where your enemy is, get at him as soon as you can, and strike him as hard as you can."

Returning to the Tennessee River, Grant moved his force upriver to Pittsburg Landing for a strike at the vital rail center in Corinth, Mississippi. Confederates under Albert Sidney Johnston attacked him first on April 6, triggering the bloody battle at Shiloh. Although nearly overrun the first day (during which Johnston was killed), Grant was reinforced that night and counterattacked on April 7, driving the Confederate army off the field. Over the next month and a half, a Union army made its intended move to successfully capture Corinth.

River navigation and cooperation with the U.S. Navy made Grant's remarkable string of successes possible. The Navy had a command structure separate from the Army's, so naval officers did not have to cooperate with their counterparts—unless they wanted to do so. To Grant's credit, he saw the Navy as an equal partner, not as a support service, and he made a point to cultivate strong working relationships with his naval peers. Those partnerships became a key component to his overall success.

And he would need all the help he could get for his next mission. To sunder the Confederacy in half, the Federal government needed to secure the "Father of Waters"—the Mississippi River. And to do that, a major Rebel bastion along the river would have to fall.

At the outbreak of war, Maj. Gen. Winfield Scott, general-in-chief of the U.S. Army, proposed a strategic plan to

▼ The Anaconda Plan was the brainchild of Union General-in-Chief Winfield Scott on how to defeat the Confederacy. His strategy offered a blockade of southern ports and an advance down the Mississippi River to cut the Confederacy in two. Many considered the plan too passive and argued this long and slow defeat of the South was like the coils of an anaconda wrapping around and suffocating its prey—hence the name of Scott's plan. (Library of Congress)

▲ This map, produced by the U.S. Army at the time of the Vicksburg campaign, shows the vicinity immediately around Vicksburg. Note such features as the line of hills that extends northeast and southwest of Vicksburg; the Yazoo River and Chickasaw Bayou; Young's Point; Millikan's Bend; and, directly opposite the city, the DeSoto Peninsula. (National Archives)

cut off the seceded states from trade and supplies. The first part of the plan included blockading major southern ports along the Atlantic coast and the Gulf of Mexico. For the second part, Scott suggested sending a force down the Mississippi River to cut the nascent Confederacy in two. Thereafter, the land armies and riverine navies would move inland, strangling the Confederacy. And thus, "the Anaconda Plan" was born.

Scott took criticism for his idea because it would require time to execute. Most younger officers expected a quick war, certainly not one what would last long enough for Scott's plan to come to fruition. Discouraged, the overweight and ill 75-year-old Scott—a veteran of the War of 1812 and Mexican War hero—retired. Events would eventually prove him—and his Anaconda Plan—to be prescient.

Aside from strangling the Confederacy, a second reason for securing the Mississippi presented itself. Confederate control of the lower river would severely hamper the economies of the states in America's "Old Northwest"—Ohio, Indiana, Illinois, Michigan, and Wisconsin. Because transportation through the Appalachians was so challenging, those states depended on the free flow of goods up and down the Mississippi river system. "The right to navigate the Mississippi River at all times is so important," said William T. Sherman, one of Grant's most trusted subordinates, "that … [it] will justify any and all measures mild and severe that will secure it."

From the south, Federals targeted New Orleans, Louisiana, the largest city in the Confederacy. From the north, they eyed Memphis, Tennessee. Midway between them, crowing high bluffs that overlooked a hairpin turn in the river, sat Vicksburg, Mississippi, which "occupied the first high ground coming close to the river below Memphis," a Union general would note. "So long as it was held by the enemy, the free navigation of the river was prevented."

Vicksburg's bluffs, steeply rising two hundred feet from the river's edge, had long attracted attention. The Natchez people had first lived along the riverbank in that region, and French explorers from New Orleans had visited as early as 1719. In 1814, a traveling Methodist minister, Newitt Vick, found the area so attractive he settled his family there, naming it "Walnut Hills." Although Vick and his wife both died of Yellow Fever in 1819, Vick's son-in-law stayed on and incorporated the town as "Vicksburg" in 1825, five years after Mississippi's statehood in 1820. The town hosted an initial population of 150 souls.

By the time of the Civil War, Vicksburg—also known as the Hill City—had become the Warren County seat and second-largest city in the state, with 3,500 White residents and another 1,500 Black residents, the vast majority of whom were enslaved. Enclaves of German, Irish, and English residents lived in town, although nearly every other European ethnicity was also represented. Northerners, Easterners, Southerners, free and enslaved Black people, and Native Americans all passed through town carried by the river, sometimes staying but usually passing through.

The city's waterfront was the busiest in the state, not only with steamboat traffic traveling north and south but rail traffic moving east and west. On the western bank of the Mississippi, the Vicksburg, Shreveport & Texas Railroad terminated at the tip of DeSoto Point, the finger of land in the middle of the river's hairpin turn. Every 30 minutes, shuttles crossed between the railroad terminus and Vicksburg's bustling waterfront, and from there, people and products could go up or down the river on steamboat, or by land to the state capital on the Southern Railroad of Mississippi at Jackson, forty-five miles east. From there, rail lines could take supplies north into Tennessee, east to Montgomery or Birmingham, or south to Mobile and the Gulf Coast.

Levee Street paralleled the river. Known as "Vicksburg-under-the-hill," this rough-and-tumble seedy part of town catered to river life. Docks and warehouses were interspersed with saloons, brothels, and

▼ A correspondent for *Harper's Weekly* noted the "abrupt and difficult ascent" of Vicksburg's hillside construction: "The town, when viewed from the opposite bank, appears as if the houses were built on terraces above one another, and the lower doors of one habitation are often-times visible over the roof of the building in its immediate front." (Library of Congress)

▶ Vicksburg was a city built on steamboat traffic. Its position midway between Memphis to the north and New Orleans to the south made it an especially ideal location for a stop. (Library of Congress)

gambling dens. A steep walk up Jackson Street—which went all the way to the state capital if you followed it that far—brought a traveler to "Vicksburg-on-the-hill." Washington Street, the main thoroughfare, was lined with shops and, thanks to steamboat transport, offered the luxuries of nearly any modern city. Vicksburg boasted six newspapers, three hotels, a theater, a tobacconist, grocers, tailors, a carriage-maker, Clarke's Literary Room, and a synagogue and several churches, including the towering steeple of St. Paul's Catholic Church. The Warren County Courthouse, with its even higher clock tower, was the tallest structure between Memphis and Baton Rouge and overlooked both town and river.

And it was all made possible by cotton. On the eve of the Civil War, Mississippi was the country's largest producer of the white staple, growing 535.1 million pounds in 1859. Vicksburg's transportation infrastructure made the city the ideal hub. If

▶ Looking northward from the city offered a view of residences and businesses, with a low-lying area known as Catfish Row closer to the river. The bend of the river around DeSoto Point is visible, as is, to the right, the beginning of the line of hills known as Walnut Hills. (Library of Congress)

"Cotton was King" across the South, it ruled from a high perch atop Vicksburg's bluffs.

The river and railroad weren't the only parts of Vicksburg's transportation network. The city sat near the southern end of the Mississippi Delta. A thousand rivulets and streams drained from the state's interior through rugged ridge land, like forks of lightning in reverse, all striking the Mississippi River. The city's position on the river near the south end of this watery network made Vicksburg a natural concentration point for the up-delta economy.

The delta was an area of "impenetrable thickets and canebrakes," the wildest and least-settled region of the state. It would be through this alluvial country that the U.S. Army would have to travel were it to continue its march south from the rail hub at Corinth in Mississippi's northeast corner. Not until the Navy captured

▲ The riverboat traffic brought people of all backgrounds to Vicksburg, making it both "Southern" and "cosmopolitan." Merchants offered nearly any sort of goods imaginable. (Library of Congress)

The River from the Hills

"From the hilltops the Mississippi is a grand object as its streams come sweeping with majestic circuit round the bend on the right, and flowing, in a line wonderfully direct for that erratic stream to the blue distance. Water always looks more beautiful when viewed from an eminence—from the heights of Vicksburg its appearance is especially charming."

— from the *Memphis Appeal*, 1859

Memphis in early June 1862 would a possible riverine avenue open itself.

There would be nothing easy when it came to taking Vicksburg. "It is the strongest place I ever saw, both by nature and art," Sherman would say later in the year, "and so far as we could observe, it is defended by a Competent form of artillery Infantry and Cavalry, besides its Rail Road connections with the interior give them great advantage."

Confederate President Jefferson Davis owned a plantation just south of Vicksburg. He understood the city's geographic importance as "the Gibraltar of the Confederacy" and described Vicksburg as the "nailhead that holds the South's two halves together." The railroad on the west bank of the river brought people and supplies from the Confederacy's supply-rich Trans-Mississippi region of Louisiana, Arkansas, and Texas. Once across, they funneled through Vicksburg to Jackson on a rail network that moved those people and supplies across the sprawling Confederacy.

U.S. President Abraham Lincoln likewise recognized Vicksburg's importance. "Vicksburg is the key!" he declared. "The war can never be brought to a close until that key is in our pocket." (Vicksburg has ever since been known as "the Key City".)

Initially, the river-savvy Grant was in no position to make a move on Vicksburg. Following the battle of Shiloh, he had been stuck in a kind of administrative limbo. He was second in command of the entire department, but his immediate superior, Maj. Gen. Henry Halleck, funneled orders around Grant rather than through him. Halleck's puzzling behavior was born out of a deep personal sense of overcautiousness and a jealousy of Grant. "My position was so embarrassing in fact that I made several applications … to be relieved," Grant later admitted. Sherman urged patience. Halleck played coy.

▼ The clocktower of the Old Court House Museum offers a beautiful view of modern Vicksburg, the Yazoo River bypass that flows in front of the city, and Walnut Hills to the north. Note how flooded the lowlands are on the opposite side of the bypass. Federal troops had to contend with similar high water throughout the early months of 1863. (Chris Mackowski)

Fate intervened in the summer of 1862 when an unrelated series of events in the Eastern Theater of the war led to Halleck's promotion to general-in-chief of the Army. Halleck replaced Maj. Gen. George B. McClellan, who had in his turn replaced the aging Winfield Scott. Known as "Old Brains" for being a thoughtful military strategist, Halleck seemed the ideal candidate for the job, particularly since he had been taking credit for Grant's string of successes. Once Halleck departed for the Eastern Theater in July 1862, Grant assumed the department's top post. Even all the way from Washington, D.C., Halleck continued his passive-aggressive handling of Grant by refusing to let him execute a strategic plan in the Western Theater.

Grant would eventually have an opportunity to make a run at Vicksburg, but it would fall to the Navy to make the first attempts. "But in the end Vicksburg must be reduced," Sherman declared in a letter, "and it is going to be a hard nut to crack."

The First Attempts at Vicksburg

The first significant opportunity to severe the Confederacy along the Mississippi came in the spring of 1862 following the fall of New Orleans in late April. "The opening of that river is the first object to be attained since the fall of New Orleans," stressed Secretary of the Navy Gideon Welles.

▼ The navy did its best to subdue Vicksburg, but as Admiral Porter concluded by the end of July, "[A]ny man of common sense would know that this place cannot be taken by ships." (*Harper's Weekly*)

Flag Officer David Farragut, the naval hero who forced the capitulation of the Crescent City, was tasked with the mission. Farragut preferred to target Mobile, Alabama, but cutting the Confederacy in two via the Mississippi offered greater strategic possibilities. Farragut didn't think the mission would take long, so he sent part of his flotilla to Mobile to prepare for operations in that area while he took eleven ships up the Mississippi. "Depend upon it," he boldly predicted, "we will keep the stampede up on them."

Farragut's squadron also included two troop transports carrying 1,500 infantrymen under the command of Brig. Gen. Thomas Williams. These men served under the overall command of Maj. Gen. Benjamin Butler, just assuming control of New Orleans after the city's fall. Williams was specifically tasked with the destruction of the Vicksburg, Shreveport & Texas Railroad, which terminated opposite Vicksburg at the tip of the DeSoto Peninsula.

The ships steamed northward on May 7 in several waves, with Capt. Thomas T. Craven of the USS *Brooklyn* leading the initial group. As the ships passed, Craven

Profile:
David Glasgow Farragut (1801–70)

David Glasgow Farragut spent his sixty-first birthday—July 5, 1862—sitting on the Mississippi River, far from the ocean he loved. Days earlier, his flagship, the *Hartford*, had run aground on a shallow sandbar, and he nearly had to abandon it. "It is a sad thing to think of leaving your ship on a mud-bank, five hundred miles from the natural element of a sailor," he wrote his wife.

As the U.S. Navy's first-ever admiral, Farragut had spent his entire career at sea. Born in 1801, he saw his first service during the War of 1812 as an eleven-year-old volunteer serving under his foster father, Commodore David Porter. Like Farragut, Porter's two oldest sons, William "Dirty Bill" and David Dixon, would pursue naval careers.

Farragut fought pirates in the Caribbean, blockaded ports in the war with Mexico, and established a naval base in the Pacific. When the Civil War broke out, he played an early instrumental role in the U.S. government's "Anaconda Plan," tasked with blockading and then capturing his childhood home of New Orleans. On April 19, he ran his fleet past two forts protecting the mouth of the Mississippi River, Fort Jackson and Fort Philip, then steamed up the river to force the surrender of New Orleans. Congress rewarded his bold initiative by promoting him to the newly created rank of rear admiral.

Later in the war, Farragut would go on to more maritime glory with the August 1864 capture of Mobile Bay—a target he had eyed on and off since the fall of New Orleans. He's best known for a defiant charge through a field of floating mines—called torpedoes—shouting, "Damn the torpedoes! Full speed ahead!" (or something like it—his exact words have been obscured by history). The victory earned him promotion to vice admiral in December 1864. He earned promotion to full admiral, the nation's first, July in 1866.

▲ David Glasgow Farragut married Susan Marchant in 1824; she died on December 27, 1840. Three years later, nearly to the day, he married Virginia Dorcas Loyall, they had one surviving son. Farragut died on August 14, 1870, at the Portsmouth Navy Yard in Kittery, Maine. He is buried in Woodlawn Cemetery in the Bronx. (Naval Heritage and History Command)

noted that the riverbanks were "thronged with people gazing in amazement, and no doubt bitterness of feeling":

> It was interesting and sometimes exciting, as we steamed along in-shore, to witness dense crowds of spectators. In front of the large sugar plantations their white occupants were collected in groups, gazing askance at us, the ladies often turning their backs upon us, showing by their manner that they would give worlds, if they had them, to be able to crush us from the face of the earth.

Slaves gathered, too, with "such demonstrations of joy, such jumping and bowing, and such antics and grins...."

Most of the ships were smaller gunboats, but several were large seafaring vessels that required deep water. They were not especially well-suited for the twists and turns, shallow channels and strong currents of brown-water operations. While the Mississippi was 100 feet deep in its main channel—and was experiencing what naval officers called "almost unprecedented high rise" that spring—the ever-changing current created hidden sandbars. "My anxiety lest the *Brooklyn* should ground on some one of these sand bars, or on some submerged levee, kept [me] constantly on my feet, and that from sunrise to sunset," Craven recalled.

The current averaged a brisk four and a half miles per hour. The river's tangled course made for constant—and sometimes tight—navigation challenges. "[O]ur vessels are too long and draw too much water," Farragut fretted. He had not been able to find enough river pilots to help guide the ships on their journey, either. "We take the boatmen who go up in the steamers or flatboats, and generally have to force them," the naval commander said, "but they know little or nothing of the river's depth or channel for vessels of our draft." The *Brooklyn* was, "on one or two occasions almost hurled by the impetuous current and eddies against the banks of the river," Craven complained.

Floating trees propelled by the strong current rocketed toward the ships. Worse, below the surface, hidden deadheads—submerged trees, ensnarled on the river bottom poking upward at sinister angles—posed an ever-present danger to wooden hulls. At night, unable to see the dangers in the water, the ships pulled close to the bank and anchored. There, they stocked up on wood or coal for their boilers and,

▶ The blue-water navy found the brown-water Mississippi a foreign and hostile environment to operate in. (Chris Mackowski)

according to Craven, endured torment by "the musquitoes [*sic*] after candlelight."

"They will keep us in this river until the vessels break down, and all the little reputation we have made has evaporated," Farragut complained. "A beautiful prospect for the 'hero' of New Orleans!" He predicted the Mississippi would "use up" the naval resources. "Fighting is nothing to the evils of the river—getting on shore, running afoul of one another, losing anchors, etc.," he wrote. Craven considered the whole affair "a wild-goose chase."

As if to prove him wrong, along the way Farragut's small fleet forced the capitulation of Baton Rouge, Louisiana, on May 9—the second capital of a Confederate state to surrender. Farther upriver, Natchez, Mississippi, surrendered three days later. Near the mouth of the Red River, midway between the two towns, the ships passed the first of several large piles of burning cotton bales stacked near the riverbank. "[A]s far as the eye can reach, we see smoke arising from other heaps," Craven said, "and as we steam along the river is filled with such cotton as could not be burned without endangering their buildings." Local plantation owners, incorrectly assuming the Federal expedition was a raid for cotton, burned their stocks to deny them to the Yankees. Many who did not voluntarily burn their cotton received unwelcome calls from Confederate guerillas, who burned their cotton for them.

On May 18, Farragut sent a three-boat squadron ahead of the main fleet. Commanded by Commander Samuel P. Lee, the gunboats demanded Vicksburg's surrender. Brigadier General Martin Luther Smith, commanding the city's garrison, declined, saying that "having been ordered here to hold these defenses, it is my intension to do so as long as in my power." Lieutenant Colonel James L. Autry, governor of the military district, refused in even more defiant terms: "Mississippians don't know, and refuse to learn, how to surrender to an enemy. If Commodore Farragut and Brigadier-General Butler can teach them, let them come and try."

Commander Lee gave Vicksburg's military leaders 24 hours to evacuate civilians and, on May 20 around 5:00 p.m., ordered the gunboat *Oneida* to fire on the city in what would be the first of thousands of rounds lobbed into the city over the next fourteen and a half months. Rebel batteries fired back and the exchange ended soon thereafter. The battle for Vicksburg had officially begun.

Incensed by the Confederates' refusal to surrender, Farragut thought the city

▼ Federal Commander Samuel P. Lee was a cousin of the famous Confederate general who commanded the Army of Northern Virginia. (Naval Heritage and History Command)

▲ Later in the war, Brig. Gen. Martin Luther Smith would serve as the chief engineer for Gen. Robert E. Lee's Army of Northern Virginia. (Library of Congress)

should be "chastised." However, arriving on the scene on May 24, he soon understood what a tall order that might be. The city sat on a series of bluffs the rose steeply from the river's edge. "[T]he place was strongly fortified by earthworks, some of their batteries being so high that it would be impossible to reach them with our guns," Craven later recounted, "and from the nature of the ground it would have been folly to attempt the landing of our troops." All the while, Confederates could rain iron down on the Federal ships as they tried to keep themselves steady in the current.

Southerners had long recognized the strength of Vicksburg's position. "The features of the surrounding country are such as to render it very strong," Confederate engineer D. B. Harris once reported, "and without any other defensive works I think any probable attack the enemy may attempt with his land forces can be repelled." Martin L. Smith, however, began creating "other defensive works," first by positioning and protecting his 18 guns so they could ward off any threat from the river. Smith also had 3,600 infantry in the city, with reinforcements on their way.

Farragut wanted to make an attempt against the city, but his subordinates urged caution. Even General Williams, tasked with destruction of the railroad,

▶ The USS *Oneida* fired the first shots in the long campaign to take Vicksburg. (Naval Heritage and History Command)

demurred. The railroad was underwater for twenty miles because of the flooded river, he pointed out, so his job was effectively done. He didn't think he had enough men to take the city. "[I]t would be impossible for me to land, and I see no chance of doing anything with the place," he said.

Farragut reluctantly agreed, realizing "it would be useless to bombard [Vicksburg], as we could not hold it if we take it." However, he predicted that within ten days, everyone would change their minds. By then, he continued, the river's falling water level and the appearance of Confederate reinforcements would make it even more difficult. Besides, he had orders from Washington to take Vicksburg and knew he would have to return.

On May 26, Farragut detailed Lee's small squadron to blockade Vicksburg and occasionally harass the city with fire. "A shell thrown in upon them occasionally will obstruct them and retard their work," Farragut suggested, "besides keeping the town in a state of siege, cramping their supplies from below and above." Then, with the rest of the fleet, he descended the river to New Orleans to refit and—now with a better idea of what it would take to capture the city—prepare for a second attempt.

Beware on the way down river, Farragut warned his ships' captains: The current could accelerate ships to as much as ten miles an hour. "They say that coming down the river is the most hazardous," he explained, "as you come with such velocity that if you run on shore, on the spits, it is extremely difficult to get off."

That wasn't the only hazard. As they passed the small town of Grand Gulf just south of Vicksburg—"the most dangerous part of the river," Farragut called it—guerillas opened fire on some of the gunboats with a piece of field artillery. When the *Brooklyn* threatened to burn the town in retaliation, townsfolk begged for leniency. According to Craven, they claimed they "were entirely at the mercy of wandering bands of freebooters [who] had come there without their consent and fired upon our troopships without the least warning." Federals tried chasing the guerillas to no avail and instead levied a penalty on the town by loading up with supplies before leaving.

As soon as Farragut got back to New Orleans, Washington barraged him with directives. "It is of paramount importance that you go up and clear the river with the upmost expedition," the Navy Department told him. "There is not a moment to be lost

▼ Commander Davis's fleet steamed south from Memphis. (Naval Heritage and History Command)

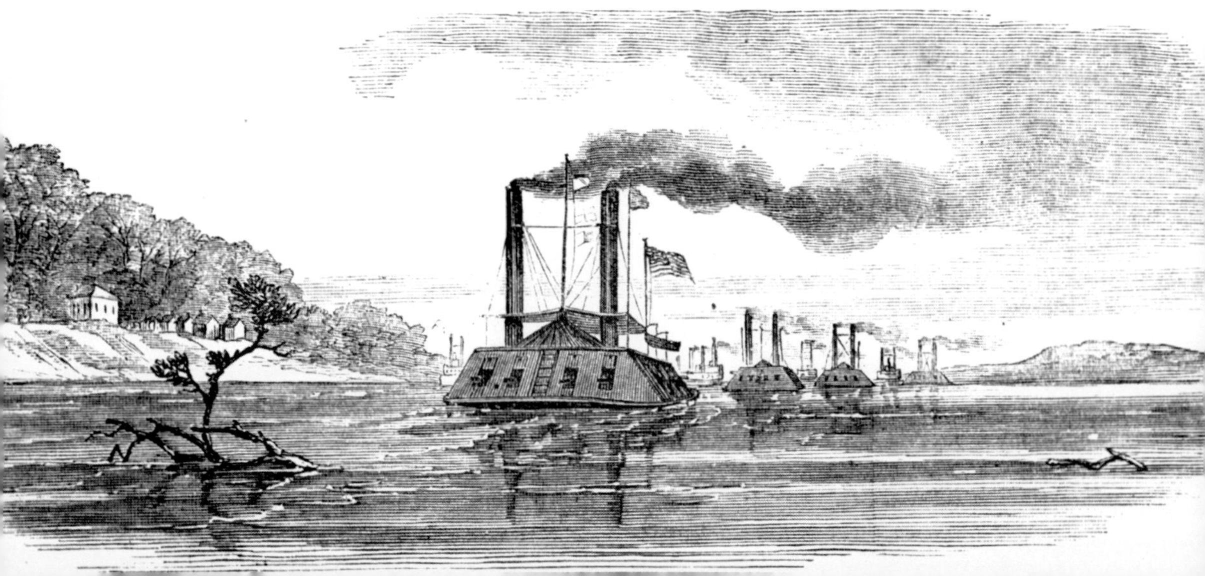

▲ "The fleet shelling the rebel batteries at Vicksburgh [*sic*], June 28, 1862." (*Harper's Weekly*)

on the Mississippi." Within three weeks Farragut again steamed upriver, this time with twenty-seven ships and gunboats augmented by the eight-boat mortar fleet of his foster brother, David Dixon Porter, recalled from their preparations off the coast of Mobile.

Thomas Williams would also bolster the fleet, this time with an increased force of 3,200 infantrymen from Connecticut, Massachusetts, Michigan, Vermont, and Wisconsin. And once the fleet got to Vicksburg, Farragut was supposed to meet a naval force commanded by his old friend, Flag Officer Charles Davis, coming down from Memphis.

The admiral worried the river's depth would drop as spring wore on. He worried about malaria and heat. He worried about the physical toll the river took on ships, tearing out anchors and cracking hulls. "[T]he whole Navy will be destroyed in twelve months" by the Mississippi's "elements of destruction," he informed Secretary of the Navy Gideon Welles. He gritted through it, though, determined to carry out his orders. Porter, for his part, admitted, "I am heartsick and fear failure up the River."

During Farragut's three weeks in New Orleans, Confederates in Vicksburg had continued improving their fortifications. The Confederates had 29 artillery pieces facing the river and more and stronger fortifications. "The batteries ... are in good condition," reported engineer D. B. Harris, "and I think capable of resisting an attack of the enemy's fleet, but I am not sure they can prevent his passing up the river if he should have the boldness to attempt it."

An additional 10,000 reinforcements had already arrived. Some were Kentuckians under former U.S. vice president and now Confederate general John C. Breckinridge. Others were Mississippians under Brigadier General Daniel Ruggles. Both officers were capable fighters. Overseeing the entire operation, superseding M. L. Smith and James L. Autry, was Maj. Gen. Earl Van Dorn. The dashing former cavalryman hailed from nearby Port Gibson, Mississippi, and was a personal friend of Confederate President Davis. Van Dorn promised to defend Vicksburg at all hazards, "even though this beautiful and devoted city should be laid in ruins and ashes."

It would be Grand Gulf that was laid in ruins and ashes first. As the fleet steamed past the town, guerillas once again opened fire. Williams put his men ashore and made good on his threat to burn the town.

Farragut's fleet arrived below Vicksburg on June 18. The next day, with no sign of the contingent from upriver, his gunboats passed the time by shelling the city. "The work is rough," Farragut admitted. "Their batteries are beyond our reach on the heights. It must be done in the daytime, as the river is too difficult to navigate by night."

They did manage one bit of night work, though. After dark on June 24, a group of sailors and Marines went ashore at Davis Bend, 15 miles south of Vicksburg. This was where Jefferson Davis and his brother, Joseph, owned the adjoining plantations Brierfield and Hurricane, respectively. The raiding party plundered both operations, making the war especially personal for the Confederate president.

◀ Foliage masked the masts of the mortar boats that accompanied Farragut's fleet. (Naval Heritage and History Command)

That same night, the gunboats from Memphis arrived and were waiting upriver. Farragut surprised everyone by deciding to run upriver past Vicksburg's batteries—something he didn't need to do but apparently did just to show he that could. In light of the relative ineffectiveness of everything else he'd been doing, a show of naval might would be good for the spirits of his men.

As the ships steamed past the city, firing as they went, Vicksburg's batteries opened on the fleet. "[T]he ridge of bluffs seemed one sheet of flame," one observer noted. Farragut successfully slipped by with eight killed, thirty-six wounded, and no ships lost.

The brown-water gunboats that awaited surprised him. "They look like great turtles," he announced. Assembled, though, the two fleets appeared to one observer like "the greatest naval force hitherto assembled at one time in the New World."

As the navy bombarded the city, Williams's brigade set to work excavating a canal across the base of DeSoto Point, the peninsula of land inside the river's hairpin turn. The idea was to create a waterway to

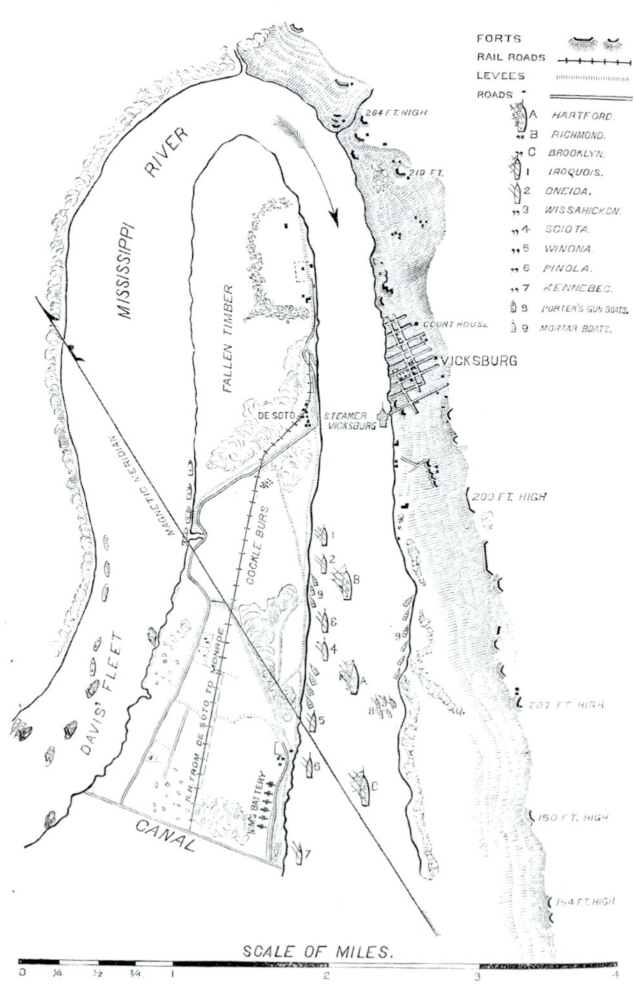

▼ Commodore Davis's flotilla converged on Vicksburg from the north to join Farragut's from the south, as illustrated by Farragut's map reproduced in Farragut's memoir. (*The Life of David Farragut*)

▶ Work on the canal started strong but soon lagged in the malarial Louisiana heat. (Naval Heritage and History Command)

bypass the hairpin turn and thus bypass Vicksburg and its commanding guns, making the so-called "Gibraltar of the Confederacy" superfluous.

The long ditch was initially set at four feet deep and five feet wide, with the expectation that the redirected Mississippi would funnel through and the erosion that resulted would widen and deepen the channel.

The effort did not go as planned. "The labor of making this cut is far greater than estimated by anybody," Williams admitted. They made steady but slow progress until part of the canal caved in at several points. That delay cost three days, during which time the level of the Mississippi fell, leaving the lip of the canal "some feet above the level of the river, the water falling faster than we could dig."

Worse, the Mississippi summer oppressed the Northerners and, working as they were in the malarial swamps and mudflats, disease ripped through their ranks. "The health of the troops has been much impaired by the absence of proper shelter," Williams rightfully complained. By July 23, two-thirds of his men were down, "thin, pale spiritless and yellow." To help them, Williams impressed as many as 1,200 slaves from nearby plantations. "They work and shout as they work, thinking they're working for their freedom," he wrote to his wife, "and if the canal is a success will deserve it and shall have it." The effort was not enough. Williams would suspend work by the end of July.

As disease decimated the infantry, so too did it ravage the sailors who were, according to one officer, "suffering dreadfully" by being cooped up in the close quarters of their ships.

Farragut's frustration grew. The combined naval forces couldn't level the city by bombardment, and they had no way to silence Confederate batteries firing at them "so long as the enemy has a large force behind the hills to prevent our landing and holding the place," he said. Besides, Williams's brigade was "too small to attack the town, or for any other purpose than a momentary assault to spike guns, should such an opportunity offer."

"[A]ny man of common sense would know that this place cannot be taken by ships," he confided to his wife.

Farragut tried to get additional infantry support. Major General Henry Halleck, then operating around Corinth, Mississippi, was a couple hundred miles to the north. On July 3, Halleck wired Farragut, "The scattered and weakened condition of my forces renders it impossible for me, at the present time, to cooperate with you." A brilliant opportunity for Federal forces evaporated because of Halleck's lack of initiative. "Had the army seconded Farragut and the Navy …" Gideon Welles later fumed, "Vicksburg would have been in our possession. Halleck is good for nothing then, nor is he now." It would be one day and a year, exactly, before Federal infantry would march into the city. As a result, Farragut lamented, "the ships were occupied with a monotonous siege, and various attempts to annoy the enemy."

The monotony soon broke, however, when a Confederate ironclad gunboat materialized from the nearby Yazoo River six miles to the north. Since Farragut's first trip north, rumors had circulated about an unfinished ironclad stashed away in the upper reaches of the Yazoo. The rumor was true, and her name was CSS *Arkansas*. Her workers in Yazoo City had been frantically laboring day and night to finish the ironclad. The boat was originally pieced together in Memphis but was sent up tributary because the Yazoo—with its narrow, twisting confines—was believed to be more defensible than the open Mississippi. On June 15, Davis finally sent a three-boat squadron to sniff it out after a tip suggested that the ironclad was nearly finished.

And indeed, it was closer to being finished than Federals realized. Davis's three boats stumbled on the *Arkansas* just as it was moving downriver. A frantic river battle ensued in which the strongest of the Federal boats, the ironclad

HARPER'S WEEKLY.
A JOURNAL OF CIVILIZATION

Vol. VI.—No. 292.] NEW YORK, SATURDAY, AUGUST 2, 1862. [SINGLE COPIES SIX CENTS. $2.50 PER YEAR IN ADVANCE.

CUTTING THE CANAL OPPOSITE VICKSBURG.—Sketched by Mr. Theodore R. Davis.—[See Next Page.]

▲ The canal project at DeSoto Point captivated people's imaginations so strongly it made the cover of *Harper's Weekly*. (*Harper's Weekly*)

▼ Mortars provided a greater upward arc for lobbing artillery shells into the city. (Naval Heritage and History Command)

▲ The USS *Carondelet* and the CSS *Arkansas* traded blows at point-blank range. The *Carondelet* got the worst of the exchange and was left dead in the water. (Naval Heritage and History Command)

▼ The CSS *Arkansas* resembled an ironclad turtle that belched smoke and cannonballs. (Naval Heritage and History Command)

Carondelet, was crippled. The other two boats fled with the damaged *Arkansas* in pursuit. It could not keep pace, explained the *Arkansas*'s Captain Isaac Brown—who had been injured in the fight—because of "the want of speed and of confidence in the engines."

When the *Arkansas* reached the Mississippi, it burst into "a forest of masts and smoke-stacks—ships, rams, iron-clads, and other gun-boats. . . ." "It seemed at a glance as if a whole navy had come to keep me away from the heroic city," Brown said, admitting "the genius of havoc could not have offered a finer view." The Federal naval vessels opened. As they converged on the damaged but dangerous ship, Brown had "the most lively realization of having steamed into a real volcano," and he set course straightaway for the protective guns of Vicksburg just downriver. "The shock of missiles striking our sides was literally continuous," he later reported.

The *Arkansas* made it to Vicksburg to the cheers of thousands of citizens lining the banks and docks. "But as she is very low in the water, and about the color of the river bank, and the night very dark, the rebel monster could not be seen and so escaped destruction," Williams

observed from his post across the river on DeSoto Point. Formidable as she was, the *Arkansas* had sustained real damage. "[W]e lay helplessly at anchor, with a disabled engine," Brown recalled. Half of the boat's crew had been killed or wounded. They spent several days on the waterfront, making repairs.

On July 22, Farragut ordered a strike against the *Arkansas* tied at its moorings. The *Essex* and the *Queen of the West*—the Federal fleet's largest ironclad and most powerful ram, respectively—made ineffectual runs at the *Arkansas*, which doled a serious blow to *Essex* in return and made *Queen of the West* run aground for a short time.

With that ignoble ending, Farragut's time in front of Vicksburg ended. Orders arrived recalling his fleet to New Orleans, where better assignments awaited. On July 24, his ships turned downriver and disappeared. Williams's men shipped out, too. On July 28, on his own initiative, Davis withdrew back north to Memphis.

As one Confederate engineer triumphantly declared, "The Yankees have entirely and completely 'skedaddled....'"

Destruction of the *Arkansas*

The CSS *Arkansas*'s short naval career ended on August 1, 1862, as a postscript to the battle of Baton Rouge. Captain Isaac N. Brown, who was not on board, recounted the scene, which involved a rematch with the USS *Essex*:

> First Lieutenant [Henry K.] Stevens could not use that tender care which his engines required, and before they completed their desperate run of three hundred miles against time, the starboard one suddenly broke down, throwing the vessel inextricably ashore. This misfortune, for which there was no present remedy, happened when the vessel was within sight of Baton Rouge. Very soon after, the *Essex* was seen approaching under full steam. Stevens, as humane as he was true and brave, finding that he could not bring a single gun to bear upon the coming foe, sent all his people over the bow ashore, remaining alone to set fire to his vessel; this he did so effectually that he had to jump from the stem into the river and save himself by swimming; and with colors flying, the gallant *Arkansas*, whose decks had never been pressed by the foot of an enemy, was blown into the air.

◄ Smoke from artillery fire helped mask the low-lying *Arkansas* as it ran the Federal gauntlet, providing much-needed cover. (Naval Heritage and History Command)

Grant's Campaign Begins

"The campaign against Vicksburg commenced on the 2nd of November," Ulysses S. Grant would declare years later when writing his memoir. Even after the passage of so much time, his declaration sounded like a sigh of relief.

For months, General Grant had been in a sort of administrative limbo. In July of 1862, his superior, General Halleck, had moved to Washington, D.C., to fill his new position as general in chief of the U.S. Army. Halleck, however, had left Grant without any explicit strategic instructions. He was "very uncommunicative," Grant later wrote, calling the next two and a half months of limbo the "most anxious period of the war" for him.

"You have never suggested to me any plan of operations in this Department," he wrote Halleck. "As situated now, with no more troops, I can do nothing but defend my positions and I do not feel at liberty to abandon any of them without first consulting you." Those positions stretched along the rail lines of northern Mississippi and west Tennessee. Since Halleck's departure, Grant had conducted a "continued defense over a large district of the country, where nearly every citizen was an enemy ready to give information of our every move." It made for nerve-wracking, if boring, work.

During that time Grant's men engaged in a number of skirmishes and small battles, but it all felt pointless. "[T]here was much fighting between small bodies of the contending armies," he later recalled, "but these encounters were dwarfed by the magnitude of the main battles so as to be now almost forgotten except by those engaged in them."

What Grant really wanted to do, he told Halleck in late October, was destroy the railroads around Corinth, Mississippi, shift toward Memphis for reinforcements, then "move down the Mississippi Central [Railroad] and cause the evacuation of Vicksburg…."

When Halleck left for Washington, he claimed in a confidential note to William T. Sherman that he had "studied out and can finish the campaign in the West." Once Halleck got to the capital, however, he seemed overwhelmed by a series of emergencies, one following on the heels of the other: the evacuation of the Army of the Potomac from the James River peninsula outside Richmond … the organization of a new Army of Virginia … a Confederate victory at Second Bull Run (Manassas) on the same battlefield of the South's first major victory of the war … a Confederate invasion into the North … the issuance of the preliminary Emancipation Proclamation … a Confederate invasion into central Kentucky. All of these distracted him from his ability to "finish the campaign in the West."

Profile: Henry Halleck (1815–72)

If anyone seemed made for war, it was Henry Wager Halleck—at least on paper.

"[V]ery quiet and studious," Halleck left a promising collegiate career when his grandfather secured him an appointment at West Point. Slightly older than his classmates, serious in demeanor, and earnest as a scholar and cadet, Halleck "viewed the world with wide-eyed staring abstraction." Classmates began calling him "Old Brains." He became a favorite of the academy's top military theoretician, Dennis Hart Mahan, and the faculty overall admired him so much that they gave him an assistant professorship while still a student, and they kept him on the faculty for a year after he graduated, teaching chemistry, engineering, and even French. He graduated third out of thirty-one in the Class of 1839.

After graduation, he became a favorite of the army's top general, Winfield Scott Hancock, who sent him to Europe to study. During the Mexican War, he served in California. He translated the work of French military theorist Henri Jomini and wrote a book of his own, *Elements of Military Art and Science* (1846), both of which reinforced his reputation as a bright military thinker.

In California, he practiced law and was deeply involved in gaining the territory its statehood. He also did much to help develop the state's infrastructure. His practice was so successful that, in 1854, he resigned his commission to pursue his legal work full time.

◄ Henry "Old Brains" Halleck was born in Westernville, New York. In 1855, he married Elizabeth Hamilton, granddaughter of Founding Father Alexander Hamilton. They had a son, Henry, in 1856. Halleck died in 1872 at age 56 and is buried in Green-Wood Cemetery in Brooklyn. (Library of Congress)

When the Civil War broke out, General Scott called Halleck east in the hope that he might serve in a highly placed post in Washington, but having been out of the army for several years, Halleck didn't have the cache for such a posting, despite Scott's endorsement. He ended up in Missouri commanding Federal forces in the Western Theater. He proved efficient at logistics—and at taking credit for the successes of subordinates like Ulysses S. Grant—but one contemporary critic said Halleck seemed "always prepared for defeat," afraid to take risks that might jeopardize his high reputation. His caution would pay off, however: in July 1862, he would be called back to Washington to serve as General-in-Chief of the Army.

Perhaps finally realizing he could not micromanage events in his former department, Halleck wired Grant back on November 3. "I approve of your plan of advancing upon the enemy as soon as you are strong enough for that purpose," he informed his subordinate. "I hope for an active campaign on the Miss. this fall."

By that time Grant had already mobilized his forces and had begun to move. Better to beg forgiveness than wait for permission, he surmised. He ordered 31,000 men—including large detachments under Maj. Gen. James McPherson and Brig. Gen. Charles S. Hamilton—to concentrate in the town of LaGrange on the Tennessee side of the Mississippi border between Corinth and Memphis. "Take three (3) days rations in Haversacks and three days in Wagons," he instructed. "Preparations should be made for repairing the Rail Road and Telegraph." Just east of LaGrange, the Memphis & Charleston Railroad and the Mississippi Central Railroad intersected at Grand Junction, which would serve as Grant's jumping-off point south.

As Federals converged on LaGrange, they freely exercised the hard hand of war, foraging and pillaging as they marched. "Our army [is] destroying everything they can, without direction," wrote reporter Franc Wilkie, "and in fact are becoming so bold that they care very little if they are detected." He predicted that such a style of warfare would "lay this country to waste." Grant issued orders to curb the destruction, and Sherman threatened to execute looters by firing squad, all to no avail.

LaGrange swelled to the size of a small city. "We covered the fields around the town with our tents, and the camp fire smoked for miles around, lighting up the sky like the lamps of a great city," recorded one soldier. The men were glad to finally be doing something, and morale soared. "I never saw the men in as good spirits and so confident as this army now appears," declared another soldier. "We are splendidly equipped and want for nothing."

The area's population—and the strain on the army's supplies—also grew because

▼ Enslaved people fled to freedom and flooded into Federal camps in consequence of the preliminary Emancipation Proclamation. (*Harper's Weekly*)

of the large number of enslaved people who sought safety with the Federals. The issuance of the preliminary Emancipation Proclamation in September had moved the front line of freedom to the front line of the war. "Orders of the government prohibits the expulsion of the negroes from the protection of the army, when they came in voluntarily," Grant wrote. "Humanity forbade allowing them to starve."

There was "such an army of them, of all ages and both sexes," that soon the sheer number of them would make it impossible for the army to move south once the time came to do so. Grant creatively solved this challenge by putting the former slaves to work in a way that allowed them to support themselves. "The plantations were all deserted; the cotton and corn were ripe," Grant noted. The government paid them to pick and gin the cotton, which the army's quartermaster sent north to sell, with proceeds going back to the government. "[A] fund was created not only sufficient to feed and clothe all … but to build them comfortable cabins, hospitals for the sick, and to supply them with many comforts they have never known before," declared Grant. "At once the freedmen became self-sustaining."

Grant placed the chaplain of the 27th Ohio, John Eaton—whom Grant rightly described as "very able" and "efficient"—in charge of the endeavor. "It was at this point, probably, where the first idea of a 'Freedman's Bureau' took its origin," Grant proudly reflected. Later in the campaign, some of the laborers would find work cutting wood for Federal steamers on the Mississippi River.

As Grant readied his infantry to move, he sent his cavalry ahead to begin scouting the countryside and probing the enemy. By November 13, Grant's troopers had proceeded twenty-five miles south to Holly Springs, Mississippi, only to discover that Confederate forces there had already pulled back to a position south of the Tallahatchie River, about halfway between

A Glimpse of Soldier Life

Seneca B. Thrall, an assistant surgeon in the 13th Iowa, captured a glimpse of soldier life for Grant's men in late 1862:

> The days are very pleasant, at noon uncomfortably warm, though morning and evening I wear my overcoat. The dust is terrible, enveloped in clouds for miles, it fills the mouth, eyes, ears and nose.... We have fresh pork, beef, chickens, sweet potatoes, geese, which the men draw along the road. It is cooked along side the road, the dust seasons it well, but nobody here pays much attention to dirt....

▼ A newspaper correspondent said of Holly Springs: "This little town, one of the prettiest and most salubrious in the State of Mississippi, was for a long time occupied by the rebel army of the Southwest. They were driven out of it [in early December], who pushed through it and on to Oxford.... It is situate[d] on the line of the Mobile and Ohio railway, and it is about twenty miles south of Grand Junction, and twenty-eight miles north of Oxford." (*Harper's Weekly*)

Holly Springs and Oxford, Mississippi. Grant had started the campaign with his own headquarters in Jackson, Tennessee, and although he would not move his infantry to Holly Springs until later in November, he had already extended his reach more than 70 miles with virtually no opposition. Still, his challenges were multiplying daily.

The most significant obstacle was his supply line, which stretched all the way from Columbia, Kentucky, south through Jackson, Tennessee, and down to Grand Junction and on to Holly Springs, which Grant chose as his forward base. From there, Grant planned to follow the Mississippi Central Railroad some 200 miles south to Jackson, Mississippi. "That was a long line (increasing in length as we moved south) to maintain in an enemy's country," Grant conceded. The country swarmed with Confederate cavalry and partisan rangers and unfriendly civilians, making the single-track supply line more tenuous the longer it stretched.

The other main challenge Grant faced—although he wasn't sure how serious it was yet—was the Confederate army that blocked the way south. Grant's forces had beaten that army at the battle of Corinth that October 3-4. Since then, Confederate authorities in Richmond had replaced the army's commander, the fallen-from-grace Maj. Gen. Earl Van Dorn, with a newly minted lieutenant general named John C. Pemberton.

Descended from a Quaker family in Philadelphia, Pemberton performed competently as a staff officer and administrator in the prewar U.S. Army. He married a Virginia girl and made his home in that state. Despite intense family pressure to keep his commission when civil war broke out, Pemberton left the army when Virginia seceded. Because of his service experience and his skill as an artillerist, he quickly rose through the ranks of the Virginia State Militia, and then the Confederate Army, until he found himself in command of a department along the southeast Atlantic coast. Pemberton's Northerner roots, stationed as he was in the "Cradle of Secession," did not endear him to the populace. His preparations and actions, while mostly militarily correct, frustrated local landowners and politicians. Jefferson Davis eventually had to transfer him. "[H]aving confidence in his ability to make the most of the means for the protection of Mississippi," Davis promoted Pemberton and sent him to the Western Theater. Van Dorn, the man Pemberton replaced, assumed control of Pemberton's departmental cavalry.

Pemberton arrived to find an army of 30,000 men in a depressed state. "This army is generally deficient in clothing, shoes, and blankets," he informed Richmond. Some 5,000 of his men lacked reliable rifled muskets. "I am terribly in want of arms," he scolded the Confederate ordnance department. Pemberton pleaded for ammunition for both small-arms and field artillery, and asked for heavy artillery to bolster new defenses being constructed along the Yazoo River. And, as was the story across the Confederacy, "more troops"—even though the men he had "suffer greatly."

Aside from this foe in his front, Grant felt trouble stirring in his rear—"friendly fire" in the form of a political major general named John McClernand. The officer, who hailed from Lincoln's home state of Illinois, had petitioned Lincoln and Secretary of War Edwin Stanton for permission to launch his own "joint military and naval expedition" down the Mississippi in an attempt to capture Vicksburg. Grant had been cut out of the

Profile: John C. Pemberton (1818–81)

John Clifford Pemberton had joined the Confederacy for love. It wasn't love for the Confederacy, though, but rather for his wife, Martha Thompson, of Norfolk, Virginia.

Pemberton attended West Point with his childhood friend George Gordon Meade, future commander of the Army of the Potomac, and graduated 27th out of 50 in the Class of 1837. Despite his northern roots, however, Pemberton "was noted for his liberal and States-rights sentiments, and for his affiliations with the young men of the South," according to friend and later-Confederate Lt. Gen. Jubal Early. "Later, he married a lady of Virginia, which made have tended to confirm his political opinions...."

◄ John C. Pemberton was born in Philadelphia, Pennsylvania. He died on July 13, 1881, and is buried in Laurel Hill Cemetery in Philadelphia—not far from his old friend, George Meade. (Library of Congress)

Pemberton served with distinction as an artillerist in the Mexican War and later fought in the Seminole Wars. Army assignments also took him to Kansas, Utah, New Mexico, and Minnesota. At the time the Civil War broke out, he had just taken a post at the Washington Arsenal in D.C.

Although two of his brothers served in the U.S. Army, Pemberton threw his lot in with his wife's home state. He earned promotions that eventually landed him a major generalship by January 1862. Placed in command of the Department of South Carolina and Georgia, with a headquarters in Charleston, he quickly earned the distrust and dislike of politically powerful critics who accused him of being "confused and uncertain about everything." Many of them worried not-so-secretly about his loyalties.

To defuse the situation, Confederate President Jefferson Davis transferred him to command of the army in Mississippi in October 1862 and promoted him to lieutenant general. Again, Pemberton failed to make a positive impression. "He is the most insignificant 'puke' I ever saw and will be very unpopular as soon as he is known," one soldier said.

Historian Douglas Southall Freeman described Pemberton as "a technically proficient soldier" if not a brilliant one, but he would soon find himself in over his head in his new Mississippi assignment.

loop on the arrangement and was initially unsure what to do, but Halleck—who liked McClernand even less than he liked Grant—urged Grant to continue onward with his overland push into Mississippi. Halleck, meanwhile, used his incredible talent for bureaucratic obfuscation to undermine McClernand every way he could.

Grant, meanwhile, absorbed an additional 20,000 reinforcements into his army and consulted with a few key allies one final time. On November 28, his army rumbled out of its camps on its grand adventure southward. In conjunction with the movement, Grant ordered Sherman, then in command of the garrison in Memphis, to move his 17,000 men south on a course parallel with Grant's. The two forces were to cross the Tallahatchie River and aim for a link-up in Abbeville, just north of Oxford, Mississippi. Grant also requested troops from Helena, Arkansas, to make a dash across the river and strike at Grenada, Mississippi, in Pemberton's rear, which "would alarm him for the safety of his communications," Sherman later said. With any luck, that might even dislodge Pemberton.

When Grant reached the Tallahatchie, however, he found the river "very high, the railroad bridge destroyed and Pemberton strongly fortified on the south side." Sherman, several miles downriver at Wyatt, similarly described the Tallahatchie as "a bold, deep stream, with a newly-constructed fort behind." As the Federal commanders soon discovered, no enemy awaited them in the far-bank fortifications. The raid on Grenada had spooked Pemberton, just as Sherman and Grant had hoped, and the Confederate commander had ordered another withdrawal, this one abandoning the Tallahatchie line. "The retreat of the Confederate Army was rapid & confused," Sherman crowed, "and the effect was equal to a Victory."

Pemberton committed a consequential blunder by withdrawing. "A crossing would have been impossible in the presence of

▼ David Dixon Porter (left) and John McClernand (right) would become key players in Grant's attempt to take Vicksburg. Originally ordered to cooperate with McClernand on an expedition down the Mississippi, Porter soon developed a strong distaste for the self-serving political general. (*Harper's Weekly*)

an enemy," Grant later admitted. Instead, Pemberton had given the enemy free passage—a decision that immediately triggered questions about his competence and loyalty. "Our soldiers were ready and anxious for a fight, and it was owing to the bad generalship … of Pemberton that we did not drive the last blue devil from the country," declared one Confederate.

Once on the south side of the river, the two Federal forces converged on Oxford. There, on December 5, Grant received a change of plan from Halleck: Grant was to hold the line with as few troops as he could while "the largest number possible is thrown upon Vicksburg with the Gunboats." Halleck hinted that this force should concentrate in Memphis and be on its way no later than December 20.

Events in Memphis with McClernand, it seemed, were coming to a head. McClernand had been personally recruiting men for his Vicksburg expedition, and they had begun converging on Memphis as their rendezvous point. McClernand himself had not yet arrived. "McClernand is announced as forming a grand army to Sweep the Mississippi when the truth is he is in Springfield Illinois trying to be elected to the U.S. Senate," Sherman snarked to his younger brother, Sen. John Sherman of Ohio. Once McClernand arrived, he would take command of the Memphis expedition and head south. If Grant reached Memphis first, he could co-opt McClernand. As Halleck cannily pointed out, "You have command of all troops sent to your department, and have permission to fight the enemy where you please." In other words, if it should happen to "please" Grant to launch his own expedition against Vicksburg with any or all of the troops then in Memphis, so be it.

Grant caught on and sent Sherman to Memphis to assume control. Grant did not want everyone milling about waiting for McClernand to arrive because he outranked Sherman and could take command. Instead, Grant planned to hold Pemberton in place while Sherman collected the troops from Memphis and went down the Mississippi "with the cooperation of the gunboat fleet under command of Flag-Officer Porter." Their objective, Grant said: "a lodgment up the Yazoo and capture Vicksburg from the rear."

Grant had already laid the groundwork for such a movement. In a meeting before his move toward Holly Springs, Porter had

Welles on Porter

On October 1, 1862, Secretary of the Navy Gideon Welles promoted David Dixon Porter to command of the gunboat squadron based in Memphis, replacing Charles Henry Davis. Welles offered a sketch of Porter in his diary entry that day:

> Porter is but a Commander. He has, however, stirring and positive qualities, is fertile in resources, has great energy, excessive and sometimes not over-scrupulous ambition, is impressed with and boastful of his own powers, given to exaggeration in relation to himself,—a Porter infirmity,—is not generous to older and superior living officers, whom he is too ready to traduce, but is kind and patronizing to favorites who are juniors, and generally to official inferiors. Is given to cliquism but is brave and daring like all his family. He has not … in his profession, though he may have personally, what the sailors admire, "luck." It is a question, with his mixture of good and bad traits, how he will succeed. His selection will be unsatisfactory to many, but his field of operation is peculiar, and a young and active officer is required for the duty to which he is assigned….

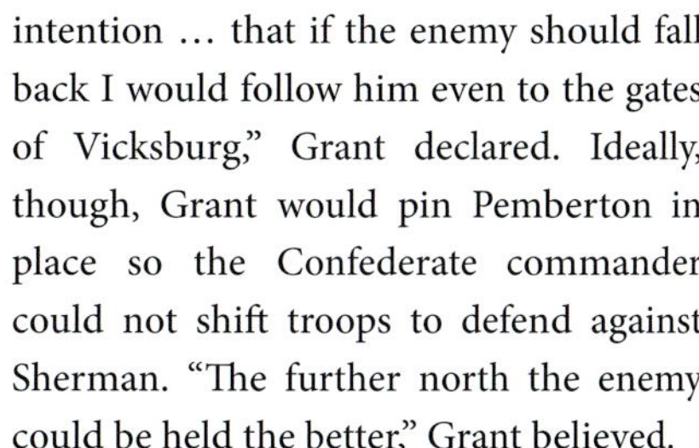

explained to Grant that his naval squadron had been ordered to Memphis to assist McClernand. But, Porter hastily added, "I am ready to cooperate with anybody and everybody." Grant had come to the naval officer as an equal, demonstrating humility rather than superiority in a move that favorably impressed Porter. The naval officer was more than willing to give Grant's plan for Sherman a try.

While Sherman moved down the river, Grant planned to move overland and engage Pemberton along the Yalobusha River near Grenada, where the Confederates had fallen back after the Federal stab from Helena. "It was my intention ... that if the enemy should fall back I would follow him even to the gates of Vicksburg," Grant declared. Ideally, though, Grant would pin Pemberton in place so the Confederate commander could not shift troops to defend against Sherman. "The further north the enemy could be held the better," Grant believed.

▼ One of the most colorful figures of the Civil War, cavalryman Nathan Bedford Forrest has been referred to as "the Wizard of the Saddle" by admirers and "that Devil Forrest" by detractors. (Emerging Civil War)

Sherman's force, meanwhile, withdrew to Memphis on December 8 while Grant eyed Pemberton's force to the south. The farther he moved south, though, the more Grant worried about "the impossibility of maintaining so long a line of road over which to draw supplies for an army moving in an enemy's country."

Then calamity struck—not once, but twice.

On December 19, a cavalry force under Maj. Gen. Nathan Bedford Forrest of the Army of Tennessee struck Jackson, Tennessee, severing the rail line with Grant's supply depot at Columbus, Kentucky. "This cut me off from all communication with the north for more than a week," Grant reported, "and it was more than two weeks before rations or forage could be issued from stores…."

A second raid the next morning proved far more impactful. Thirty-five miles behind Grant, Confederate cavalryman Earl Van Dorn led a 3,500-man force in a dawn raid against Grant's forward supply base at Holly Springs. Van Dorn captured the 1,500-man garrison commanded by Col. Robert C. Murphy of the 8th Wisconsin. "The capture was a disgraceful one to the officer commanding but not to the troops under him," Grant declared. Over the course of eight hours, Van Dorn's horsemen engaged in a saturnalia of destruction, burning heaps of supplies and destroying the railroad. Leaving town, they headed north, tearing up more railroad as they went before riding to safety.

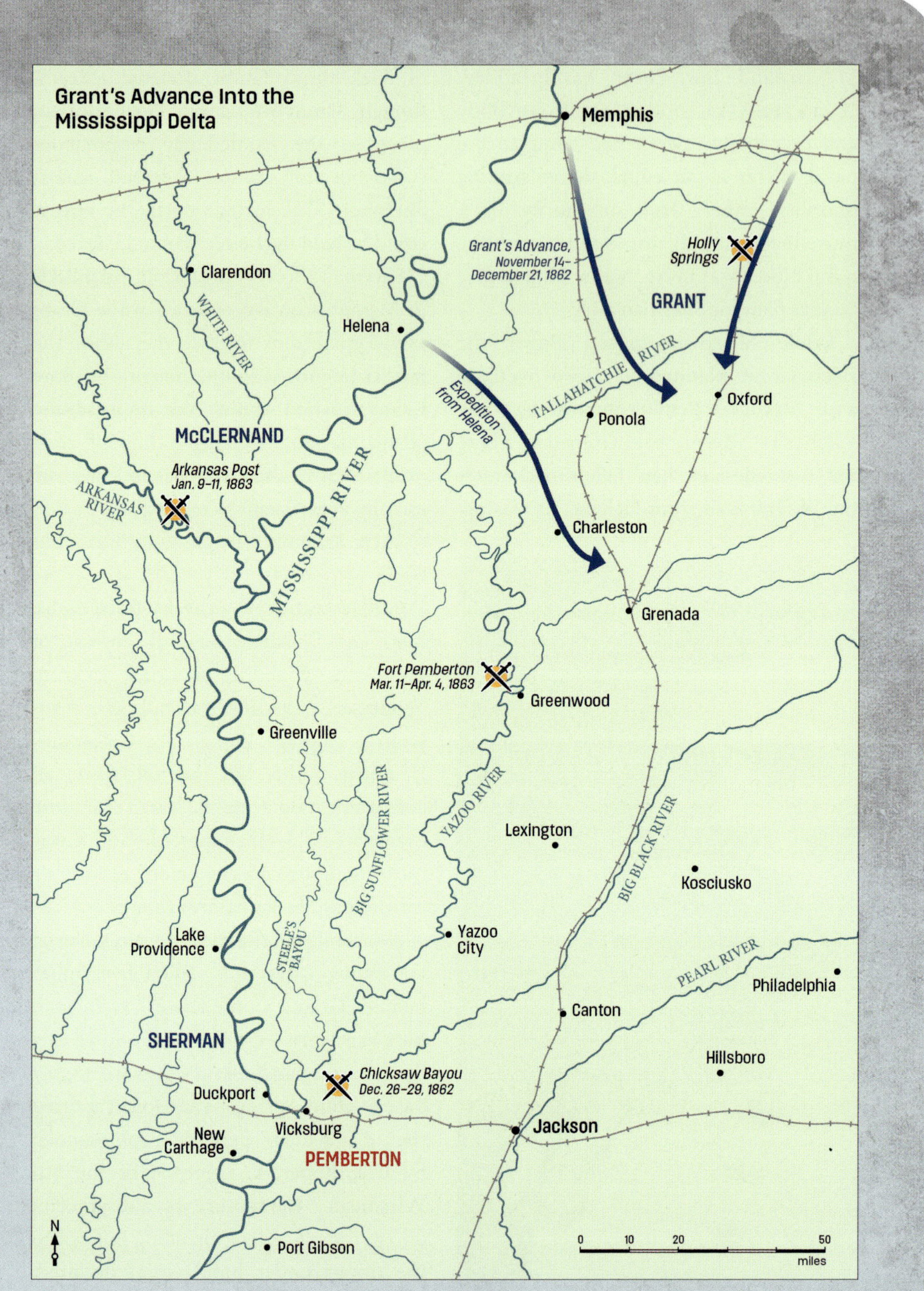

▲ Grant initially advanced south from Memphis, Tennessee, with a feint to support him from Helena, Arkansas. A Confederate hit on his supply base at Holly Springs forced his withdrawal. In the following months, Federals made several attacks along the Mississippi and its adjacent waterways.

► Earl Van Dorn would eventually meet an early end not because of battlefield exploits but because of personal indiscretions. He would be murdered by a jealous husband in May 1863. (*Photographic History of the Civil War*)

Of the two hits on his supply line, "The surrender of Holly Springs was more reprehensible," Grant admitted. "Our loss of supplies was great at Holly Springs," he reported, "but it was more than compensated for by those [we had] taken from the country and by the lesson taught." The lesson? "[W]e could have subsisted off the country for two months instead of two weeks." Grant would apply that lesson later in the campaign.

News of Grant's supply woes "caused much rejoicing among the people remaining in Oxford," he recounted.

"They came with broad smiles on their faces, indicating intense joy."

"What are you going to do now without anything for your soldiers to eat?" they asked in self-satisfied tones.

"I'm not disturbed," Grant replied. "I've already sent troops and wagons to collection all the food and forage they can find for fifteen miles on each side of the road."

Countenances fell. "What are we to do?"

The unfazed Grant continued. "We endeavored to feed ourselves from our own northern resources while visiting you. Your friends in gray have been uncivil enough to destroy what we had brought along, and you can't expect men, with arms in their hands, to starve in the midst of plenty. Perhaps," he added, "you should emigrate east, or west, fifteen miles and assist in eating up what we leave."

The destruction of Holly Springs, however, forced Grant to terminate his offensive. He marched his force back north, his landward push toward Vicksburg at an end before it ever really got started.

Chickasaw Bayou

"Memphis is the now the best and most complete base of operations on the Mississippi," Sherman declared in late November prior to his move with General Grant into the Magnolia State. "[T]roops can be raised, organized, fed, and equipped better than at any place I have ever seen." And those troops, he noticed, had a harder attitude to them—they were "full of the idea of a more vigorous prosecution of the war, meaning destruction and plunder." He expected them to take that harder-nosed attitude into battle.

Sherman was, even then, "ready to move inland, down the river, or anywhere."

His move inland in support of Grant had proved a false start. On December 12, however, he was back at his Memphis headquarters hatching his next plan. With still no sign of McClernand, Sherman was eager to scoop up that officer's newly recruited troops, add them to his own, and strike out for Vicksburg. When David

◀ Walnut Hills, also known as Chickasaw Bluffs, would become infamous as "Where Sherman Failed." (Library of Congress)

▲ The cooperation between army and navy would be crucial throughout the Vicksburg campaign. (*Harper's Weekly*)

D. Porter arrived with naval assets, the two officers solidified arrangements for a riverine expedition down the Mississippi.

Rather than attack the city directly, they decided to navigate up the Yazoo River, which provided a way to get at Vicksburg from the back side. "With the Yazoo open to us, our land forces could disembark on its east bank on the same ridge which forms the bluff of Walnut Hills at Vicksburg," Sherman wrote. Porter sent a reconnaissance force in advance to find the best spot for the army to land. The rest of the fleet would follow and, taking advantage of "the latest and most authentic information from naval officers," Sherman planned to "land our whole force … and then … reach the point where the Vicksburg & Jackson Railroad crosses the Big Black; after which to attack Vicksburg by land, while the gunboats assail it *by water.*"

Sherman expected to encounter Vicksburg's garrison of infantry somewhere along the way, but with Grant holding the bulk of Pemberton's troops in place along the Yalobusha River, he did not expect much trouble. "[T]he presence of this force acting in concert with Grant must produce good results," Sherman insisted to his senator brother. This would be the elder Sherman's first independent combat command, and he tried to cover his excitement by managing expectations. "[D]on't expect me to achieve miracles," he warned—although he undoubtedly hoped for some. "The move is one of vast importance and if successful will remove the chief obstacles to the navigation of the Mississippi, although it will as long as war lasts be a source of Contention."

Also hovering over the expedition—unspoken but clearly recognized—was the pressure exerted by the Emancipation Proclamation, set to officially go into effect on January 1, 1863. To have teeth, the measure needed combat victories. "I wish [Gen. Ambrose] Burnside and [Gen. William] Rosecrans were getting along faster," grumped Sherman to his brother, "but I suppose they encounter the same troubles we all do." Sherman had apparently not yet learned that Burnside's Army of the Potomac had been badly beaten at Fredericksburg, Virginia, on December 13. William S. Rosecrans, meanwhile, was trying to button down final logistics before sallying out of Nashville into central Tennessee. Expectations were high for Grant's army to achieve victory.

Sherman finally departed Memphis on December 20 with 20,000 infantrymen

Sinking of the *Cairo*

Named for Cairo, Illinois (pronounced "KAY-row"), the USS *Cairo* was one of seven original ironclads built for brown-water operations along the Mississippi. Admiral David Dixon Porter, commander of the squadron, called it "one of my best."

In preparation for a Federal riverine operation against Vicksburg, the *Cairo* was one of several ships detailed to travel up the Yazoo River north of the city and sweep for torpedoes, thus clearing the way for the invasion force. The torpedoes—what we would today call "mines"—were crude devices that floated just under the service and had to be manually detonated by observers onshore.

On December 12, 1862, the Cairo bumped up against one such mine, and Confederates detonated the mine. The explosion momentarily lifted the ironclad out of the river, and then water began to pour into the gaping hole blown into the gunboat's front left hull (the "port bow" in sailor terms). The boat went down in 12 minutes, although another boat in the fleet, the ram *Queen of the West*, picked up survivors. Miraculously, no one was killed in the blast; six sailors were injured.

Salvaged in 1960, the *Cairo* now rests on display at Vicksburg National Military Park, where a museum displays artifacts recovered from the wreck.

◀ The USS *Cairo* (Library of Congress)

◀ The restored remains of the *Cairo* are on display in an outdoor pavilion in Vicksburg National Military Park. (Chris Mackowski)

loaded onto 67 transport steamers, escorted by three of Porter's gunboats. Hours before departure, Sherman had heard an unconfirmed rumor about the attack on Holly Springs. As a result, he would make his attack unsupported by Grant to the north. Van Dorn's raid, coupled with Grant's withdrawal, allowed Pemberton to shift forces south to meet Sherman's arrival.

Sherman's flotilla stopped in Helena, Arkansas, that night to take on more troops. It took two days for everyone to load up and concentrate, but by December 23 the small armada was moving south once more. When guerillas harassed the Federals, Sherman's men retaliated by burning any structure used to house the enemy fire. "Thus the rebels gave us considerable to do," observed one soldier, "and the consequence was, that soon the whole river was lined by burning dwellings and plantations. Nevertheless the rebels persisted in their useless and to themselves so destructive mode of fighting…."

▼ William T. Sherman proved to be Grant's stoutest defender, even when he disagreed with his commander. Their partnership had been forged in the crucible of rumor. "Grant stood by me when I was crazy, and I stood by him when he was drunk," Sherman said, "and now we stand by each other." (Library of Congress)

On Christmas Eve, the expedition made a brief stop near DeSoto Point so troops could spend Christmas morning destroying, once again, the railroad that connected the Trans-Mississippi Theater with Vicksburg. This side excursion tipped off the Confederates to the Federal presence and gave the Vicksburg forces an extra day to mobilize, prepare positions, and call for reinforcements from other parts of the state. Word reached Maj. Gen. Martin Luther Smith, commander of the Vicksburg garrison, while he was attending a social event in his honor. "This ball is at an end," he announced grimly. "The enemy are coming down the river. All non-combatants must leave the city."

Smith placed Brig. Gen. Stephen Dill Lee in charge of the defense. The 29-year-old artillerist was a recent arrival in Mississippi from E. Lee's Army of Northern Virginia. This Lee, recorded one admirer, "a splendid, handsome six footer, was always universally popular every where, was a natural-born soldier, & was one of the few young men who afterward deservedly rose by hard fighting to the rank of lieut. gen…." Lee had 3,000 men under his command: the 17th Louisiana, the 26th Louisiana, and two companies of the 46th Mississippi, plus two artillery batteries under Capt. Jeffery L. Wofford. Confederates rushed out to fortify the area with "directions to hold the enemy in the bottom to the last and give time for re-enforcements to arrive," said Smith, who put out the call for those additional troops.

Porter made similar good use of the extra time by sending a patrol up the Yazoo to gather the latest intelligence and find a possible landing point for Sherman's three infantry divisions. Unfortunately, the news there wasn't good: mines blocked the waterway downriver of Haynes Bluff, the preferred landing point. The best Porter could do was transport the infantry up the Yazoo 12 miles to the former site of Johnson's plantation—which the U.S. Navy had burned on a previous occasion—to the banks of a stream called Chickasaw Bayou. The thought of moving through that watery region of gloom discouraged Sherman. "The country between Yazoo and Mississippi is of black vegetable mold, full of streams and bayous, and exceedingly impracticable in wet and wintry weather," he said. There were few roads, and "a few hours rain renders the roads impassable to artillery."

With the specter of a failed mission hanging over his head, and the knowledge that General McClernand would soon arrive and supersede him in command, Sherman gave a reluctant go-ahead. On December 26, Porter's fleet led Federal forces upriver and unloaded them. Frederick Steele's division disembarked above the mouth of the bayou, George

▲ After the war, Stephen Dill Lee would return to Vicksburg as one of the first commissioners for Vicksburg National Military Park and play a hugely influential role in the park's development. (Library of Congress)

◀ This *Harper's Weekly* diagram shows how Confederate torpedoes operated. Too much river debris prevented effective use of self-detonating mines. (*Harper's Weekly*)

Washington Morgan's near the ruins of Johnson's plantation and Morgan Smith's close by. Andrew Jackson "Whiskey" Smith's division, which would not arrive until the next night because of its railroad-wrecking mission, would disembark just below Morgan Smith's.

Federals could see before them a heavily forested area broken by patches of cypress swamp and cane brakes, and some two miles distant, a broken ridge of hills—the same ridge of hills Vicksburg sat on. The stretch of the ridgeline immediately to their front was called Walnut Hills. "[A] continuous obstacle 12 miles long, formed of abatis and water, skirted the base of the hills and but a short distance from them," Martin Luther Smith would explain in his after-action report. The moat-like skirt of water along the base of the hills formed the branches of Chickasaw Bayou, which converged into a "Y" that drained northwest into the Yazoo River.

▼ The cedar-lined channel of Chickasaw Bayou looks much today as it did in 1862. (Chris Mackowski)

Sherman offered an overawed description of the Confederate position. He wrote that his men occupied "an insular space of low boggy ground with innumerable bayous or deep sloughs." Beyond "was an irregular strip or bench of table land, on which was constructed a series of rifle-pits and batteries, and behind that a high, abrupt range of hills, whose scarred sides were marked all the way up with rifle-trenches, and the crowns of the principal hills presented heavy batteries."

In fact, Confederate works in no way resembled that description when Sherman first arrived because the hills were hardly fortified at all and only lightly defended. Whether Sherman exaggerated in his report as a way to explain away what happened, or whether his experience there was so brutal that the image of the final fortifications seared themselves into his mind, is hard to say. "Nevertheless," he harumphed, "that bayou with its levee parapet, backed by the lines of rifle pits, batteries, and frowning hill, had to be passed before we could reach *terra firma* and meet our enemy on anything like fair terms."

Three roads crossed the swampland. One, from Johnson's plantation, ran directly to Vicksburg, but, said Sherman, "it crossed numerous bayous and deep swamps by bridges, which had been destroyed" and so offered no clear advantage. Another paralleled the west side of Chickasaw Bayou itself, passing from Johnson's plantation to a plantation owned by Mrs. Annie E. Lake; Lee characterized this as "a good road," and it crossed the bayou on a corduroy bridge. The third, on the east side of the bayou, meandered along a cypress swamp and a standing body of backwater called Lake Thompson. Pemberton, in his report of the action, complimented the intelligence work of Porter's navy because "the enemy [showed] accurate knowledge of all the approaches."

As the other divisions disembarked, Morgan advanced his column down the road toward Mrs. Lake's. Heavy skirmishing erupted around the plantation's corn cribs, which "had been completely commanded by [Federal] sharpshooters," said Col. William T. Withers of the 1st Mississippi Light Artillery, who was in command of a provisional brigade and that part of the field. Confederates finally fired the buildings to prevent further sniping. Federals fell back and settled in for the night. Colonel Withers occupied the Lake house as his headquarters.

Lee would later argue the Federals lost their best opportunity for victory at Vicksburg. "Had Sherman moved a little faster after landing, or made his attack at the mound [Sherman's bluff, or sand-bar], or at any point between the bayou and Vicksburg, he could have gone into the city," insisted the brigadier. "As it was, he virtually attacked at the apex of a triangle while I held the base and parts of the two sides."

On the morning of the 27th, Sherman ordered his divisions under Steele, Morgan, and Morgan Smith to cautiously advance in unison. Two columns converged on the Lake plantation, flushing out Withers and his hunkered-down men. The Rebels fell back under artillery cover. Two companies from the 26th Louisiana, however, crossed one of the bayou's tributaries and positioned themselves in the timber along the bank. From there, they could fire on the Federal flank. Colonel John F. DeCourcy's Federal brigade, marching in

◀ Roads were few and far between in the bottomlands around Chickasaw Bayou. The modern road today follows the historic roadbed. (Chris Mackowski)

the lead, took hours to dislodge the "stout resistance," finally charging the woods and flushing them out. By then, DeCourcy was close enough to clearly see the enemy works.

A half-mile to the right of Morgan's column, a brigade under Frank Blair and Morgan Smith's division pushed forward. The 55th Illinois and 58th Ohio, sent ahead on reconnaissance, had to cross a water obstacle using a fallen tree and officers had to swim their horses across. Several hundred skirmishers from the 31st Louisiana waited on the far side supported by an artillery piece ensconced on an old Indian Mound. Smith sent the full brigade of Brig. Gen. David Stuart to help the two regiments. "[O]ur troops were received by a very heavy volley of musketry," recalled Stuart, whose men opened in return, prompting "a sharp fire [that] was kept up till dark."

▶ The Indian Mound today is hard to find, obscured by thick vegetation. (Chris Mackowski)

▲ Chickasaw Bayou provided good channels of navigation for army transports, but note the steepness of the banks and width of the waterway—imposing obstacles for infantry. (Library of Congress)

On the left flank of the Federal formation, Frederick Steele's division found itself isolated. Confederates had cut down trees across the road running atop a levee. Steele's men had to clear it as they advanced in order to bring along their artillery. "We soon came to deep water on the right side of the levee," Steele reported, "which turned out to be Thompson's Lake instead of Chickasaw Bayou." Confederate resistance in Steele's front stopped the division for the night, which went into camp without fires.

Sherman seemed content to feel out the situation without pushing too hard. This passivity gave the Confederates more time to strengthen their position, and that evening three additional Confederate brigades arrived on the field. The new arrangement put Stephen Lee on the right, Brig. Gen. Seth Barton in the center, and Brig. Gen. John C. Vaughn on the left. Brigadier General John Gregg's brigade, held in reserve, would ultimately slide to the front between Barton and Vaughn. Additional Confederate reinforcements were mobilizing and moving toward the beleaguered hills, including 4,000 men from Pemberton's force in Grenada who were no longer held in place by Grant.

Sherman, meanwhile, benefitted from the return of Whiskey Smith's division, back from its foray against the railroad. Now at full strength, Sherman adopted a more aggressive attitude. Fog settled in overnight, covering the Confederates as they shifted dispositions and shielding the Federals as they prepared for an early morning advance.

On Sherman's left, the day opened briskly for Steele—almost at once. As his pioneers continued to clear away the felled timbers, Confederate skirmishers fired on them. Artillerists tried to drive out the Rebels, to no avail. Artillerists and pioneers alike "were subjected to a murderous fire and the pioneers either killed or wounded." Reconnaissance showed the Confederate position "so well chosen that it soon became apparent that we could neither dislodge them nor force our way along the levee without a frightful destruction of life," Steele reported. Matters only grew worse when they found themselves subject to enfilading artillery fire. Sherman eventually ordered Steele to withdraw his men, circle around, and join the rest of the army on the other side of Chickasaw Bayou.

George Washington Morgan used the morning fog of the 28th to deploy the 7th Battery, Michigan Light Artillery, in position to soften up the Confederate line in front of DeCourcy's men. For two hours, Capt. Charles Lanphere's battery hammered away. "Our fire from this position was less effective than it would have been had it not been for a lagoon at the edge of the woods, upon the opposite bank of which there was a low levee which prevented the depressing of our guns as much as was desired," Lanphere wrote. By late morning, DeCourcy and his artillerists advanced but quickly came under "a most galling fire." The Michiganders swung their gun into action again, this time "in the very face of the enemy." This attracted counterbattery fire, but support from DeCourcy's men allowed Lanphere's men to advance farther. The First Wisconsin Battery advanced to help, as well. "Here the bursting of shells, the crashing of trees, the thunder of our own guns, and the showering of bullets seemed enough almost to drive us back," admitted Wisconsinite Jacob Foster, "but bravely did our men stand their ground." The two batteries spent the rest of the day in their forward positions, working without food or rest.

DeCourcy's Indianans, Ohioans, and Kentuckians, meanwhile, fought back and forth with Col. Allen Thomas's heavily outnumbered 29th Louisiana, which managed to bottleneck not just DeCourcy's brigade, but Morgan's entire division.

▼ Federals did their best to get artillery into the action, but the limited roads and wet terrain made it a challenge. (*Battles & Leaders of the Civil War*)

Other Federal thrusts met with similar resistance. On the east side of Chickasaw Bayou, Col. Lionel Sheldon's brigade was delayed by the 26th Louisiana. Frank Blair's brigade got shuffled around, looking for an opening but finally just replacing Sheldon's men on the field.

Morgan Smith, trying to push against the Confederate position near the Indian Mound, took a bullet to the hip that knocked him out of the fight. "Poor Morgan Smith will die I fear," Sherman lamented after the battle. "His wound was partly an accidental one, but the ball lodged near his spine and I fear will prove mortal." Smith, whom Sherman called "one of my best and most daring leaders," would survive and return to command prior to the October 1863 battles for Chattanooga.

▲ A state historical marker provides the only modern indication that a battle once took place at the base of the Chickasaw bluffs. The tree-covered bluffs themselves can be seen in the distance. (Chris Mackowski)

Brigadier General David Stuart assumed temporary command of Smith's division, but Whiskey Smith arrived and, under Sherman's order, assumed control. Sherman wanted the division to attack in support of an assault by Morgan. But as Stuart said to Smith, "I considered the crossing as utterly impracticable at that point in face of the enemy's defenses, that while we might (but not without considerable and perhaps serious loss) gain the opposite shore[,] we could not possibly ascend the bank." Work continued in order to clear the way, but night fell before any advance could happen—which was just as well, because no assault by Morgan materialized. DeCourcy's lone brigade was it.

So ended December 28. The Federals managed modest gains against stubborn and effective Confederate resistance. Sherman gained a new appreciation for the tangled country, but the bayou still had lessons to dole out. Overnight, Morgan tried to move his troops across a particularly wide and deep part of the bayou by building a pontoon bridge, only to discover by dawn that he'd bridged "instead of the lake, a wide and deep slough, parallel to the bluff and filled with water." Morgan blamed the mistake on the "intensely dark" night. His men tried again in the morning, but activity drew Lee's attention to a weak spot in his line that Morgan had hoped to target.

Sherman rode out to reconnoiter the position. "The first step was to make a lodgment on the foot-hills and bluffs abreast of our position," he later said. He directed Morgan to carry the hills with a frontal assault across the corduroy bridge, with Steele to support him and hold the country road. The divisions under Whiskey Smith in front of the Indian Mound would "cross on the sand-spit, undermine the steep bank of the bayou on the farther side, and carry at all events the levee parapet and first line of rifle-pits, to prevent a concentration on Morgan." Gunboats would add to the demonstrations upriver.

The conversation that followed was debated by the key participants for years thereafter. Sherman pointed to the road past Mrs. Lake's and announced to Morgan, "That's the road to take."

In Sherman's retelling, Morgan replied, "General, in ten minutes after you give the signal I'll be upon those hills." Morgan, for his part, never shared that part of the conversation. Instead, he said one of Sherman's aides showed up with a follow-up message: "Tell Morgan to give the signal for the assault; that we will lose 5,000 men before we take Vicksburg, and may as well lose them here as anywhere else."

"We will lose the men," Morgan replied, "but from this position we will not take Vicksburg."

Morgan sent three brigades—DeCourcy's, Thayer's, and Blair's—against the Confederate right while two others circled to the right to try and pierce the seam between the Confederate right and center. "[T]hey rushed to the assault and were mowed down by a storm of shells, grape and canister, and minie-balls which swept our front like a hurricane of fire ..." Morgan reported. "[T]he assault was as valiant as it was hopeless."

On the far left of the Federal attack, Blair—the only officer on horseback—urged his men onward. They "rushed with impetuosity to the attack," the brigade commander later reported, first pushing through a growth of cottonwoods that had been chopped down and left "to form a perfect net to entangle the feet of the assaulting party. Passing through this and coming to that part of the bayou containing water, it was deep and miry, and when this was crossed we encountered a steep bank on the side of the enemy at least 10 feet high, covered with a strong abatis and crowned with rifle pits from end to end."

"These formidable works, defended by a strong force of desperate men ... would seem to require almost superhuman efforts to capture," Blair concluded.

Amazingly, with a loud huzzah Blair's men carried the forward rifle pits and, with rapidly thinning ranks, advanced toward the main Confederate works "only to pour out their lives at their base," lamented Blair. "[M]eeting a severe cross-fire of artillery," Sherman observed, the brigade "was staggered and gradually fell back."

DeCourcy's men likewise carried the rifle pits in front of them, but a crossfire caught them, as did Confederate artillery fire from the rear. Only a portion of his men made it across the bayou, dashing along the gauntlet of the road to get there. DeCourcy braved Confederate fire to direct his other regiments ahead, but even as they started across the bridge he noticed that "the destructive fire from all sides ... kept mowing down the ranks." He called his men back, using his final regiment, the 42nd Ohio, to cover their retreat.

Brigadier General John M. Thayer's brigade, assigned to assist in the assault, lent only the 4th Iowa, which deployed just as DeCourcy's men fell back. Thayer sent them forward nonetheless into a melee with the 42nd Georgia and the 29th Louisiana, assuming the rest of the brigade would soon be storming in as support. "[T]o my amazement none were to be seen and none were coming," an incredulous Thayer reported. The other Iowa regiments had been mistakenly led off the field due to a miscommunication from Steele. Thayer scrambled for other reinforcements, including the 42nd Ohio, but could find none. "I ordered and begged them, but without effect," he admitted. He was compelled to bring the 4th Iowa back.

Federal efforts at the Indian Mound also met with repulse. "The enemy made five efforts to take the breastworks by storm," wrote Confederate General Barton, "three times gained the crest of the parapet, once made a lodgment and attempted to mine, but on every occasion was repulsed with heavy loss."

The "attempt to mine" described by Barton was actually a desperate act of self-preservation by men of the 6th Missouri, who found themselves in "circumstances that called for all the individual courage for which that admirable regiment is justly famous," Sherman recounted. The Missourians had made it across the bayou but could not ascend the steep bank topped by rifle pits and an artillery battery. "The men of the Sixth Missouri actually scooped out with their hands caves in the bank, which sheltered them against the fire of the enemy, who, right over their heads, held their muskets outside the parapet vertically, and fired down," Sherman wrote. Behind them, sharpshooters from the 13th U.S. Infantry posted "behind legs, stumps, and trees, on our side of the bayou" provided what cover they could. "So critical was the position," said Sherman, "that we could not recall the men till after dark, and then one at a time."

As night settled over the battlefield, Confederates sent out parties that scooped up 21 officers, 311 enlisted men, four battle flags, and 500 stands of arms. Some 80 wounded Federals were evacuated to Vicksburg hospitals, and a flag of truce the next morning allowed Sherman's men to collect the rest. Historian Thomas A. Livermore, the eventual calculator of *Numbers and Losses in the Civil War in America*, recorded Federal losses at 1,776 (208 killed, 1,005 wounded, and 563 missing) and Confederate casualties at only 207 (63 killed, 134 wounded, and 10 missing).

▼ Fighting around the Indian Mound, shown here, was especially fierce. (*Harper's Weekly*)

▶ Pinned against an embankment with Confederates right above them, the men of the 6th Missouri tried to burrow into the dirt for protection. (*Harper's Weekly*)

Meanwhile, more Confederate reinforcements arrived including Maj. Gen. Carter Stevenson, who by seniority took over field command from S. D. Lee. "[W]e could hear the whistles of the trains arriving in Vicksburg, could see battalions of men marching up toward Haines's Bluff, and taking post at all points in our front," Sherman reported.

▼ The detritus of battle includes a destroyed artillery piece and, if you look closely enough, a human body. (Library of Congress)

A cold rain started to fall. Sherman, alone, pacing in restless strides, took stock of the day. One brigade, Col. William J. Landrum's on the far right, was "in plain view of the city of Vicksburg," but that was as close as anyone could get. "Our loss had been pretty heavy, and we had accomplished nothing, and had inflicted little loss on our enemy," admitted Sherman. He would later lay blame for the failed assault on Morgan, who "was supposed to lead his division in person" but did not. "Had he used with skill and boldness one of his brigades, in addition to that of Blair's, he could have made a lodgment on the bluff, which would have opened the door for our whole force to follow," Sherman groused in his memoirs.

Privately, he admitted to his wife that perhaps his army had dodged a bullet. "I would have pushed the attack to the bitter end but even had we reached the City unassisted we could not have held it if they were at liberty to reinforce from the interior," he confided. To his brother, Sherman wrote that he'd "pushed the

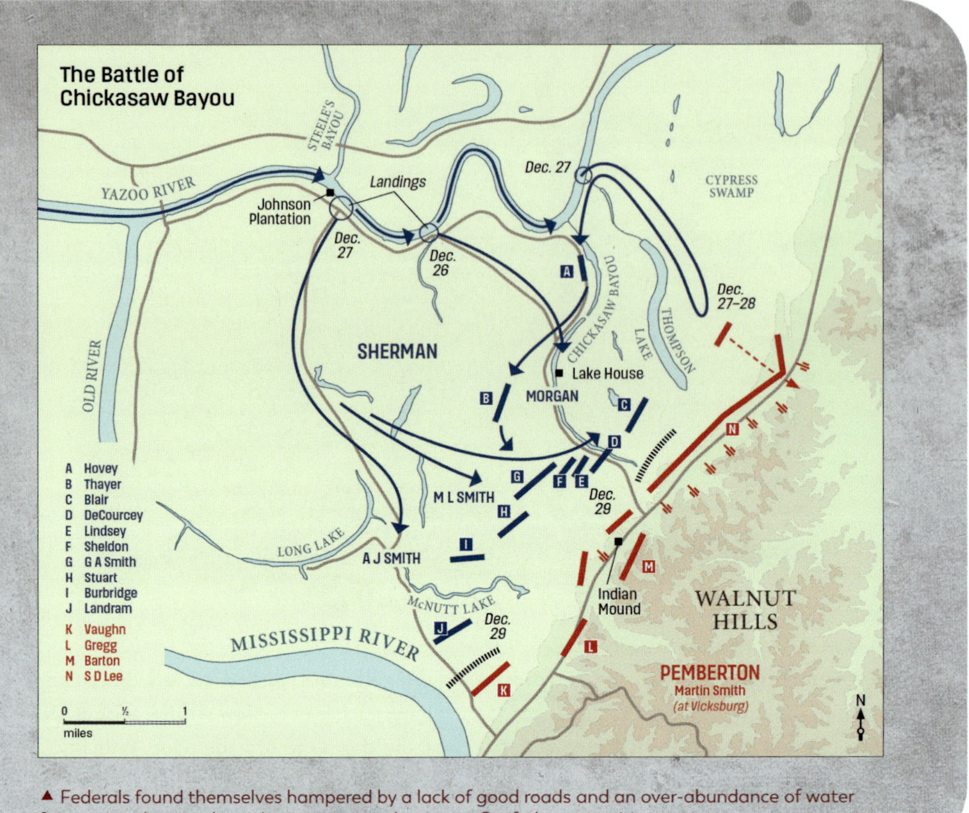

▲ Federals found themselves hampered by a lack of good roads and an over-abundance of water features as they tried to advance against the strong Confederate position.

attack as far as prudence would justify," but "was met at every point by Batteries & Rifle pits that we could not pass."

December 30 and 31 passed with skirmishing trading shots while Confederates improved their fortifications. On New Year's Eve, Sherman tried moving Steele's division up the Yazoo (which naval vessels had been mine-sweeping), for an attack on Haynes Bluff. Overnight, "the fog had settled down on the river so thick and impenetrable, that it was simply impossible to move," Sherman groused.

The fog lifted only to be replaced by torrential rain. Most of the army was camped in low swampy areas, and as if in epiphany, men began to notice "the trees bore water-marks ten feet above our heads." These and other factors convinced Sherman "that the part of wisdom was to withdraw."

"[W]e have been to Vicksburg, and it was too much for us, and we have backed out," Sherman wrote to his wife. "For five days we were thundering away" against "an enterprising & successful enemy." The Confederate position, by nature and design, was such that "no human beings could have crossed the Bayou & live." His first independent command had failed, and although he tried to put a happy face on it, he felt the weight of what that loss meant for him personally, and for the national government's newly issued Emancipation Proclamation.

"It will in the end cost us at least ten thousand lives to take Vicksburg," he concluded.

Difficulties of a Working General

General Sherman withdrew from the Yazoo River on January 2, 1863, to find Major General John McClernand waiting for him. The political general, who was mad about General-in-Chief Henry Halleck's efforts to outmaneuver him, had steamed from Memphis on his headquarters boat, the *Tigress*, to supersede Sherman in command of the expeditionary force. He brought with him the unwelcome news that Ulysses S. Grant's supply line had come to grief, and that Grant was not coming to Sherman's rescue.

The 50-year-old McClernand was a former member of Congress from Illinois. Although a friend of Abraham Lincoln's, it was McClernand's position as a pro-Union Democrat that made him a particularly valuable political ally for the president and earned him his brigadier general's commission. He served under Grant through the early part of the war, demonstrating some fighting ability despite having no formal military training. He grew to resent "West Pointers" because they did not make him feel particularly welcome.

By October 1862, McClernand was on leave in Washington, D.C., which allowed him to accompany President Lincoln on a visit to the Army of the Potomac on the Antietam battlefield in Maryland. He returned to Illinois on a mission to recruit more soldiers for what he hoped would be an independent command down the Mississippi River.

McClernand had a gift for political maneuvering—which was one reason professional officers didn't like him—and he took advantage of his connection with Lincoln to communicate directly and freely (and sometimes, without discretion) to the president. This practice earned him the ire of General Halleck, whom McClernand finally came to recognize—belatedly for the Mississippi expedition—as "my personal enemy and senselessly so." Alas, Rebel Maj. Gen. Nathan Bedford Forrest's December 18 raid against Jackson, Tennessee, played as much a role in McClernand's delay as Halleck's sleight of hand. Forrest's raid cut Federal communications and slowed the arrival of McClernand's orders.

"I am not relieved from duty here so that I may go forward and receive orders from General Grant," McClernand fumed in a message to Secretary of War Edwin Stanton on December 23 from Springfield, Illinois. "Please order me forward," he

◂ John McClernand (right) poses with President Lincoln and Army of the Potomac Intelligence Chief Alan Pinkerton during an October 1862 visit to the Antietam battlefield. (Library of Congress)

pleaded. Stanton sent his approval later that same day. As eager as McClernand was to get to the front, he delayed his trip another three days to attend to personal business. On the day after Christmas, he married Minerva Dunlop, his late wife's 26-year-old sister.

McClernand and his bride didn't arrive in Memphis until the 28th, well after Sherman had whisked away with McClernand's men for his ill-fated effort at Chickasaw Bayou. "[E]ither through the intention of the General in Chief or a strange occurrence of accidents …" he whined to Stanton, "I have been deprived of the command that has been committed to me."

McClernand hustled downriver as quickly as he could to snatch his troops back from Sherman, who he began to undercut almost immediately. In his recap of the debacle at Chickasaw Bayou, McClernand described Sherman as "a brave and meritorious officer" but added, with weasel words, "I would not detract anything from him, but give him all credit for good purposes, which unfortunately failed in execution."

McClernand withdrew the small army to Milliken's Bend several miles upriver and reorganized it into the new "Army of the Mississippi." The command consisted of two corps: one under Sherman and the other led by Maj. Gen. George Washington Morgan. Morgan's wing consisted of his own division and that of Whiskey Smith's; Sherman's consisted of Steele's division and Stuart's (formerly Morgan Smith's). Sherman would later lament that his "relief" from command, "on the heels of a failure, raised the usual cry, at the North, of 'repulse, failure, and bungling.'"

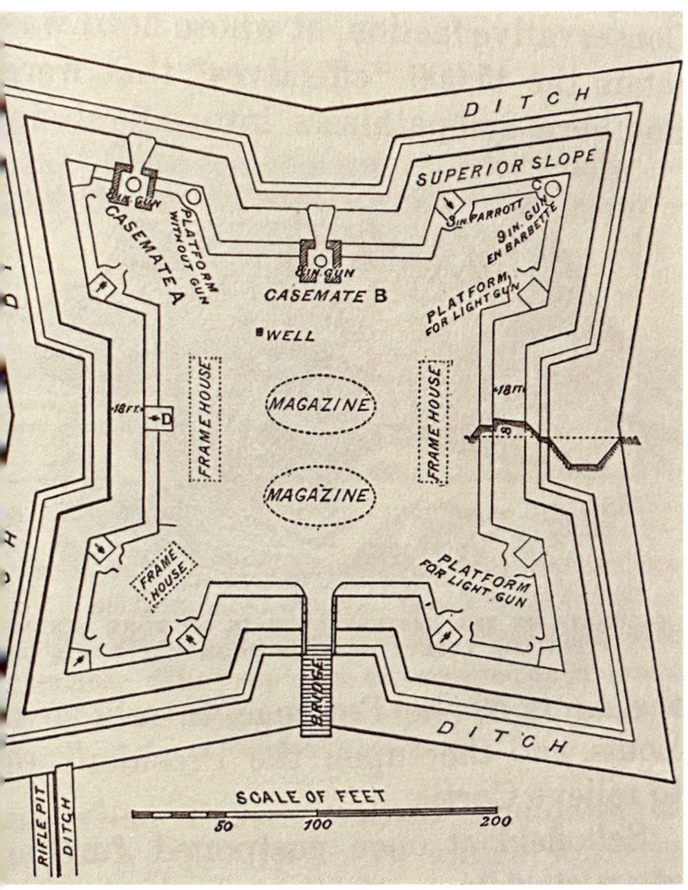

The entire thing was a bitter pill for Sherman, who found McClernand "one of the most objectionable" general officers because he possessed a "gnawing and craving appetite for personal fame and notoriety." Yet Sherman had recently told his U.S. Senator brother, John, "The President … has the right and ought to regulate all matters of command." That chicken had come home to an unhappy roost with this particular choice.

McClernand wanted to make the most of his command opportunity and find a quick victory, which would both underscore his superiority to Sherman in the field, and cement his place in command of the new small army. To do so, he set his sights on Fort Hindman, a small Confederate post about twenty-five miles up the Arkansas

◀ Fort Hindman was constructed as a typical "star fort." Crews used the dirt from the surrounding ditch (which acted like a castle moat) to build the walls. (*Battles & Leaders of the Civil War*)

▼ A map from the *Official Records* shows the terrain around Arkansas Post. (*Officials Record of the War of the Rebellion*)

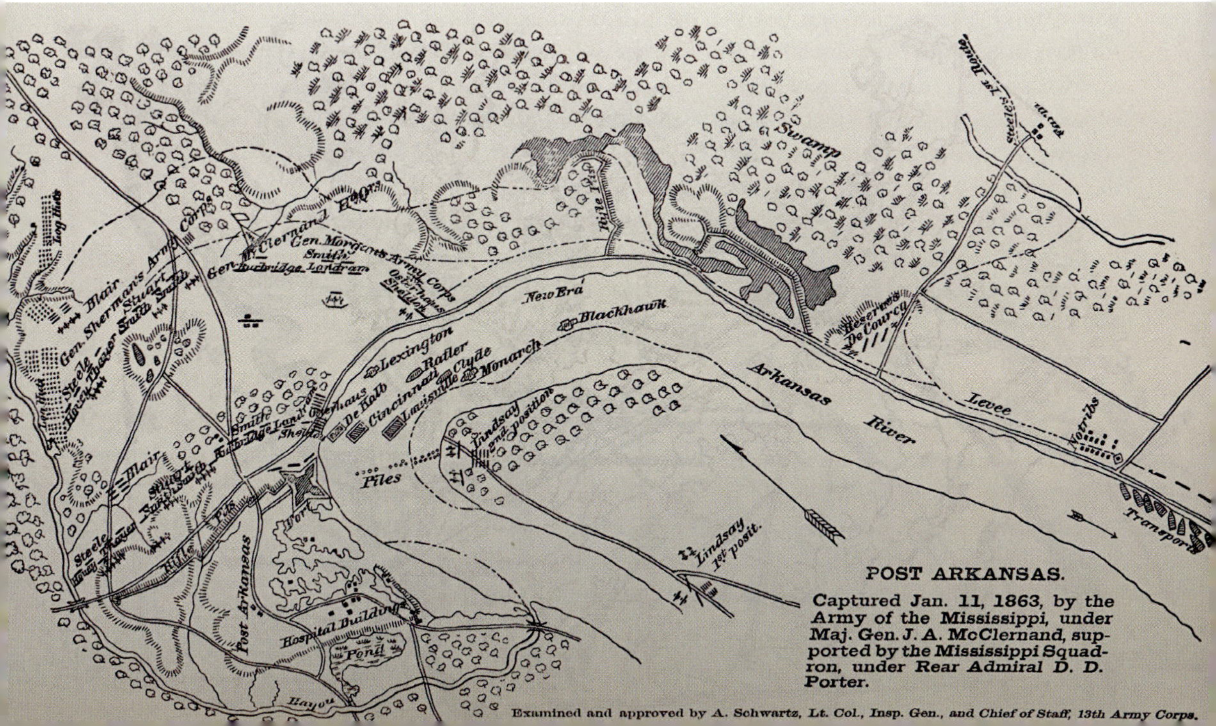

POST ARKANSAS.

Captured Jan. 11, 1863, by the Army of the Mississippi, under Maj. Gen. J. A. McClernand, supported by the Mississippi Squadron, under Rear Admiral D. D. Porter.

Examined and approved by A. Schwartz, Lt. Col., Insp. Gen., and Chief of Staff, 13th Army Corps.

River. On December 20, a Confederate raider had zoomed down from the fort and snatched the Federal steamboat *Blue Wing*, which was towing coal barges and carrying ammunition and mail. Because of this, Sherman wrote his wife, "I have no doubt some curious Lieutenant has read your letters to me."

The small fort, referred to as "the Post of Arkansas" or "Arkansas Post," was garrisoned about five thousand men and commanded passage of the river. However, Sherman had intelligence to suggest it would be "easy of capture from the rear." If so, the fall of the fort would open the waterway Arkansas all the way to Little Rock 117 miles upriver, although Sherman and McClernand both wisely focused more on the fort's threat to operations along the Mississippi. It would be "unwise to leave such a force on our rear and flank," Sherman believed, because the enemy would threaten supplies moving south from Memphis and interrupt the effort to take Vicksburg.

Sherman and McClernand conferred with Admiral David Dixon Porter in what proved to be a tense encounter because the Navy man had taken an instant dislike to McClernand. Sherman soothed the admiral's pique by assuring him the Navy's cooperation would ensure the success of the enterprise. McClernand, meanwhile, suggested that General Grant again try to move through Mississippi's interior and march upon Vicksburg from the rear—well away from McClernand's otherwise-independent command on the river.

On January 5, Porter's gunboats, including three ironclads, accompanied McClernand's infantry up the Arkansas River, an expeditionary force of thirty-three thousand soldiers and sailors. Word of the movement reached enemy ears on January 9, not long before the fleet itself arrived. Confederate Brig. Gen. Thomas Churchill and his three brigades reacted by withdrawing as much of their supplies as they could into the fort and extending its land-side defenses. Churchill also sent a plea for reinforcements to his department commander, Lt. Gen. Theophilus Holmes, who told Churchill to "hold out until help arrived or until all are dead."

Federal infantry disembarked on January 9 but did not immediately attack. Federal gunboats shelled the Confederate fort on the 10th as McClernand maneuvered his men and brought artillery onto the field, unable to find an opening. Churchill, meanwhile, extended a line of earthworks westward from the side of the fort to anchor on a stream called Post Bayou. Aside from a single company of Texas Rangers, hoped-for reinforcements from Holmes never arrived because Holmes never sent any.

▲ Brig. Gen. Thomas James Churchill would survive the war to become Arkansas's 13th governor. (*Photographic History of the Civil War*)

At 1:00 p.m. on January 11, the ironclads opened a particularly heavy bombardment from close range. Field artillery opened in concert. Thirty minutes later, the infantry moved forward. For some three hours entrenched Confederates—many armed with only double-barreled shotguns—held off their Federal counterparts. "My great hope was to keep them in check until night," Churchill reported, "and then, if re-enforcements did not reach me, cut my way out."

The naval bombardment proved too much, and the fort's walls began to crumble. Counterbattery fire slackened and fell silent, which allowed the warships to steam upriver past the fort and rake the Confederate infantry from the rear.

Confusion and casualties led to capitulation, prompting Confederates to argue over who issued the order to surrender, or whether anyone had issued such an order at all. The point was moot, Sherman retorted to Churchill and his subordinates before pointing out that many of the Confederate infantry had already been disarmed. "I was forced to the humiliating necessity of surrendering the balance of the command," Churchill admitted. Nearly 4,800 of his men ended up as prisoners, with an additional 60 killed and 80 wounded—about 25 percent of all Confederate forces in Arkansas. McClernand listed 134 killed, 989 wounded, and 29 missing.

"[M]y troops had the fighting and did the work, but of course others will claim the merit and Glory," complained Sherman. "It was not a Battle but a clear little 'affaire,' success perfect." Indeed, that night he came upon McClernand on his command boat exclaiming "Glorious! Glorious! My star is ever in the ascendant!" McClernand's report barely mentioned the Navy's decisive role in the affair, although he did send a note to Porter congratulating him for his "brilliant and efficient part...." In similar fashion, Porter skipped over McClernand's role in his own report.

McClernand mulled his future options while his men leveled rifle pits, removed stores, and burned long rows of log houses

▼ On a bluff overlooking a bend in the Arkansas River, Fort Hindman occupied a dominant position. (*Harper's Weekly*)

▼ Naval supremacy forced the capitulation of Fort Hindman. (Library of Congress)

the Confederates had built for their winter quarters. They even "found in the magazine the very ammunition which had been sent for us in the Blue Wing, which was secured and afterward used," recorded Sherman.

McClernand decided his next move was a raid up the Arkansas River and began drawing up plans for a deeper strike. He sent Sherman's corps to Helena, Arkansas, to refit. Grant nixed the idea when word arrived they were to concentrate on Vicksburg. Grant thought from the outset that the expedition to Arkansas Post was a frivolous distraction and potential waste of men and time. The move, he informed Halleck, was "a wild-goose chase." Only later, after Sherman told Grant the idea had been partially his, did Grant change his tune.

McClernand withdrew from the Arkansas River on January 18, 1863, to find Grant waiting for him. By that time Halleck had authorized Grant "to relieve General McClernand from command against the expedition against Vicksburg" and give the expedition to Sherman or take direct control himself. Grant took direct control.

It wasn't long before McClernand began to chaff against the new arrangement. "I am invested, by order of the Secretary of War, indorsed by the President, and by order of the President communicated to you by the General-in-Chief, with the command of all the forces operating on the Mississippi River ..." he informed Grant, in an effort to get the general to back down in the face of all that political weight.

Post-Arkansas Post

"All the prisoners and materials of war captured testify to the harmonious and successful co-operation of the land and naval forces, and that each nobly emulated the other in the time of patriotic duty."

— Maj. Gen. John A. McClernand

◀ The naval bombardment leveled Fort Hindman; Federal infantry finished the job after the fort's surrender so Confederates could not use the fort again. (*Harper's Weekly*)

▲ Dr. Haller Nutt was a prominent cotton planter who owned several estates across the region, including Winter Quarters. The house on the property was spared thanks to the pro-Union sympathies of the Nutts and the plantation overseer securing letters of protection from Union troops. Now, it is the only plantation home still standing on Lake St. Joseph, the rest being burned by General Sherman's troops on the march to cross the Mississippi River. (John Castaldo)

Grant smacked aside his veiled threat with General Order 13, which reiterated his role as commander of the entire department, with department headquarters "with the expedition." Tension between the two officers would remain a bedeviling influence on operations for months.

Grant had plenty else to wrestle with during the opening months of 1863. On December 17, 1862, just before Forrest and Van Dorn struck his supply lines, Grant had issued General Order 11. Ever after it has been considered his most infamous act as a military or public figure. The order stated, "The Jews, as a class, violating every regulation of trade established by the Treasury Department, and also Department orders, are hereby expelled from the Department."

It took a couple weeks for word of the order to make its way back to Washington. Once it did, President Lincoln—through Halleck—reacted immediately. "If such an order has been issued, it will be immediately revoked," declared the General-in-Chief on January 4. As Halleck later explained, "in terms proscribing an entire religious class, some of whom are fighting in our ranks, the President deemed it necessary to revoke it."

General Order 11 would dog Grant for the rest of his career. It would even become a campaign issue during his 1868 run for the presidency. "I do not pretend to sustain the order," he wrote a Jewish supporter:

> At the time of its publication I was insensed by a reprimand received from Washington for permitting acts which the Jews, within my lines, were engaged in. There were many others within my lines equally bad with the worst of them.... The order was made and sent out, by without any reflection, and without thinking of the Jews as a sect or race to themselves, but simply as the persons who had succesfully ... violated an order.... I have no prejudice against sect or race but want each individual to be judged by his own merit. Order No. 11 does not sustain this statement, I admit, but then I do not sustain that order.

In January 1863, Grant did not have time for such a succinct explanation or apology. Even as Halleck's note arrived, Grant was dealing with ongoing Confederate cavalry raids, a possible threat against Corinth, the return of Brig. Gen. James McPherson's column from Abbeville, Mississippi, and the dismal news of Sherman's bloody repulse at Chickasaw Bayou. The flurry of alarm in the wake of Sherman's defeat seems to have spared Grant from any serious fallout from General Order 11, which he obediently revoked on January 7.

While General Order 11 was a self-inflicted wound, Grant had others trying to wound him as well. One of his subordinates, Maj. Gen. Charles S. Hamilton, sent a letter to his friend, Sen. James R. Doolittle of Wisconsin, accusing Grant of being a drunkard. "He tries to let liquor alone," Hamilton confided, "but he cannot resist the temptation always." Hamilton recounted a November incident where Grant "was beastly drunk, utterly incapable of doing anything." He closed his letter by claiming to be a "warm friend" of Grant's. In fact, Hamilton bore a grudge toward Grant for promoting McPherson to corps command instead of him.

Grant had other critics who made similar accusations, some of which made it all the way to the White House. Unsurprisingly, McClernand was involved in encouraging at least one such report. Secretary of the Treasury Salmon P. Chase argued that it was not "safe or prudent" to ignore such stories, but Lincoln seemed content to let matters be so long as Grant continued to show initiative and aggressiveness. When pressed, Lincoln finally urged a group of Grant's detractors to find out what brand of whiskey Grant used. "[F]or if it made fighting generals like Grant," Lincoln concluded, "I would like to get some of it for distribution."

Grant's drinking has long been a source of speculation, with no definitive evidence to prove whether he drank to excess or not. Such rumors, however, had dogged him since his time in the Old Army, and he could not shake them now—not when critics and enemies found such low-hanging rhetorical fruit so easy to pluck. "No man's military career in the army is more open to destructive criticism than Grant's," one newspaper editor opined. A possible explanation was that Grant, a man of slight build—5'8" and 135 pounds—could not handle alcohol well, so even a single drink had an exaggerated effect on him.

Because of the lack of progress getting to Vicksburg, newspaper reporters and editors would grow increasingly critical of Grant during the first three months of 1863. Sherman's conflict with a reporter from the influential *New York Herald* further complicated the situation. The imbroglio infuriated Sherman, who

▶ *Harper's Weekly* summed up Grant's many woes in the early months of 1863: "Difficulties of a Working General Among the Bayous." (*Harper's Weekly*)

went so far as to have the reporter court-martialed—an unusual step because civilians were outside the jurisdiction of military courts. As might be expected, the press pool bound together in defense of one of their own, which led to further negative ink about Grant's thus far failed operations against Vicksburg.

Public opinion likewise turned sour, not just against Grant but against the entire struggling war effort. Northern anti-war agitators known as "Copperheads" grew "more and more insolent in their gibes and denunciation of the cause and those engaged in it," complained Grant, all the while clamoring for a peace settlement.

Meanwhile, desertion in the Army increased, driven by flagging morale, miserable weather, rampant disease, and no pay. "For five months the paymaster with his iron chest had not been seen," complained a member of the 55th Illinois, "and not only men and officers, but their families suffered many discomforts by consequence." Camped as Grant's army was on the Louisiana bank of the Mississippi River, however, deserters had few places to desert to, with rising waters trapping the men on increasingly small pieces of land.

◀ Brothers Cadwallader and Elihu Washburne played interconnected roles in Grant's operations, the former as a subordinate and the latter as an advocate, although their direct pipeline to each other sometimes worked against Grant's purposes. (Library of Congress)

"The water was very high and the rains were incessant," Grant wrote of those sodden weeks. "There seemed no possibility of a land movement before the end of March or later...." Would the Northern public wait that long? Would Lincoln? *Could* Lincoln?

"This campaign is being badly mismanaged," grumped Maj. Gen. Cadwallader Washburne, the brother of Grant's political patron, Congressman Elihu Washburne. The congressman passed the letter on to the president with some reluctance. "I fear a calamity before Vicksburg. All Grant's schemes have failed. He knows that he has got to do something or off goes his head."

Grant *was* trying. He realized "it would not do to lie idle all the time." Inactivity would demoralize the troops and further degrade their health. And so, given his situation, no sooner had Grant withdrawn his army from the Arkansas River than he began the first of what would be several efforts to get at, around, or behind, the nearly impregnable Hill City.

Waterways to Nowhere

Brigadier General Thomas Williams began his canal project on the DeSoto Peninsula with high hopes in the summer of 1862. The brigade commander's goal was to cut a ditch across the peninsula so the force of the river could break through and widen it, providing a means for the Union vessels to bypass the powerful Vicksburg batteries.

"Happily the excavation we have made is a mighty ditch," explained Williams, who led a brigade some 3,000-strong, "and the earth thrown up a respectable parapet which can be turned to military purposes if necessary." The project turned into a long and fruitless fatal toil for his infantry and the 1,200 slaves Williams pressed into service to help them. "My hopes … surrounded as I am by the sick and desponding, sometimes do give way," he admitted.

He and his troops had "entertained hopes of accomplishing in the Cutoff, something worth suffering for, and as long as that prospect was before us, officers and men kept back disease by the mere force of resolution." But failure loomed up,

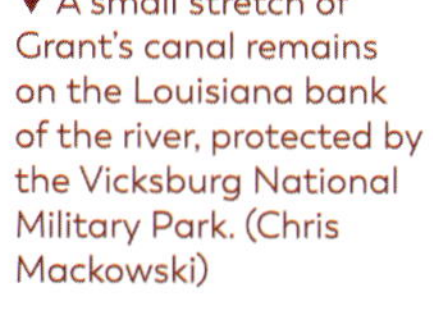

▼ A small stretch of Grant's canal remains on the Louisiana bank of the river, protected by the Vicksburg National Military Park. (Chris Mackowski)

resolution crumbled, and all the suffering was for naught.

President Lincoln had not forgotten about the project. "The President is exceedingly anxious that a canal, from which practical and useful results would follow, should be cut through the peninsula opposite Vicksburg," Secretary of Navy Gideon Welles wrote to Porter. As Grant later explained, "Mr. Lincoln had navigated the Mississippi in his younger days and understood well its tendency to change its channel, in places, from time to time. He set much store accordingly by this canal."

Thus on January 21, 1863, Ulysses S. Grant ferried William T. Sherman's corps to Young's Point, LA, just upriver of the DeSoto Peninsula, to resume work on Williams's abandoned canal. "It's no bigger than a plantation ditch," announced an incredulous Sherman when he first set eyes on it.

Engineers had surveyed the "ditch" for Grant earlier in the month. It was about six-foot deep and between nine- to twelve-foot wide. Trees choked the banks, both ends of the canal were in slack water, and the canal's lower mouth was susceptible to enfilading fire by the Confederates. The ditch needed to be widened and, to truly harness the power of the Mississippi, the mouth of the canal had to be moved upriver to "receive the stream where it impinges against the shore with the greatest velocity," concluded Grant. Such a location would take better advantage of a more powerful current so that the river itself could help scour the canal deeper and wider.

Confederates across the river watched all the sudden activity with keen interest. "They doubtless design another effort at the canal," one observer noted, "but they will have to go through an average depth of 20 feet of blue clay for two miles before the father of waters will co-operate in the nefarious experiment. In the meantime, their labor may be disturbed." As ominous as that last prediction sounded, Federals

▼ The canal required an incredible amount of engineering expertise and physical exertion. (National Park Service)

▲ A sketch on the 9th Connecticut monument at Grant's Canal depicts the workers' lives of woe. (Chris Mackowski)

were mostly beyond the reach of any Confederate interference, at least for the time being.

On the Louisiana bank, white tents dotted the sodden fields and campfires sprung up along the levee lining the west side of the canal. Transport boats hugged the shore at anchor. "I have not much faith in the Scheme," Sherman honestly admitted to his wife, "though I will do all I can to help it." John McClernand's corps, assigned to help the mammoth effort, camped a few miles above at Milliken's Bend.

DeSoto Point could not have been less hospitable. The excessive rains and unusual floods made the "unctuous earth" swampy and soft and "questionable." "[T]he swamps became lakes, and camps and roads were sloughs of black mire," one soldier complained, clearly voicing the opinions of many other comrades. Everywhere else there was nothing but mud. "The driest place I could find to sleep last night the mud was four inches deep," wrote one Iowan.

Soldiers dug wells that offered clear, but contaminated, drinking water. Disease spread quickly and death followed. "The men, although now hardened campaigners, working day after day mid-leg deep in mud and water, in a malarious

▶ The army did not have enough dry land to keep up with the number of men who died each day. They resorted to burying men on the levees. (*Battles & Leaders of the Civil War*)

▲ *Samson*, one of the two steamers used to open Grant's canal to the Mississippi, soon came under Confederate fire. (*Frank Leslie's Illustrated Weekly*)

climate, under various discouragements and lack of generous food, gradually lost spirits, grumbled audibly, and began to fail in health," observed an Illinois soldier.

As many as 85 men died each day. Burial parties interred them along the outside of the levee, which was usually the only dry ground available. High waters sometimes washed bodies out of their shallow graves. As the canal project stretched on over time and camps flooded in high water, men moved onto the levee among the macabre company of the dead.

Grant charged Capt. Frederick E. Prime, his chief engineer, with overseeing the canal project. Prime quickly concluded the men needed proper tools, the work teams needed a schedule, and the project needed a dredge. Prime eventually secured a pair of dredges dubbed, appropriately enough, *Samson* and *Hercules*. Soon, wrote Grant, they were "doing the work of thousands of men."

That may have been a lower bar than Grant realized. His infantry showed little enthusiasm for their task. "I have never seen men work more grudgingly," complained Sherman. To supplement their labor, Captain Prime pressed into service a number of the local Black men who had worked on the canal back in the summer. Like Sherman, though, Prime noted "a want of energy and indifference on the part of the contrabands."

Even after more shovels and picks and wheelbarrows arrived, the toil remained backbreaking. The gray clay did not give way easily, either to the new tools or the river itself, which spilled into the canal from either end and from cracks in the levee—but did little to scour the channel deeper. Standing water made the work even more challenging, and submerged stumps made the work more hazardous. Prime employed pumps to help clear the water, but the pumps had trouble keeping up with the brown water.

The weather and river both remained mercurial. Prime's correspondence reflected the capricious conditions: "little or nothing done—rain" … "at work—favorable weather" … "no work—rain, and high water" … "a fine day; wind from the northwest, and mud drying rapidly" … "No work outside of the main levees, on account of high water and the river still rising." In January and February, temperatures sometimes dropped below freezing, and snow flurried. At other times, as was recalled by an Ohioan, "electric storms here were something terrific," and offered "fearful" lightning that made it dangerous to carry a rifle—men stuck their firearms, bayonet down, into the earth.

Prime worried constantly about the Mississippi's water level, which would, literally, make or break the project. "Should circumstances require the expedition to remain here for some length of time, and the river continues to rise, there will be much trouble from the backwater in the swamps coming from the *crevasses* in the levee," he explained. His worry soon enough came true. Instead of cutting a deeper channel, the increasing volume of water in the canal overflowed its banks and flooded the camps. Sherman's headquarters eventually "had the water all around it, and could only be reached by a plank-walk from the levee, built on posts." Other officers kept their headquarters on nearby boats. "[T]he canal won't do," growled the corps commander in a letter to his wife. It was "a pure waste of human labor."

Grant had come to this conclusion by early February. "I lost faith in its ever leading to any practical results," he said of the canal. If there was any bright side to the project, it's that "Our labors … have had the effect of making the enemy divide his forces and spread their big guns over a great deal of territory." That was little consolation for canal workers when, on February 16, Confederates began firing toward the southern outlet of the new channel. Eventually, the Rebels had guns in position large enough to fire into the lower end of the canal itself—which instantly made the canal untenable as a bypass.

Grant, however, did not call off construction. Succeed or fail, he needed to keep busy, not just for the sake of his men but for the sake of appearances. "It was apparent that continued activity was the only condition on which he could hold his position," an aide later commented. Sherman summed it succinctly: "During the months of January and February, we

▼ A levee kept most of the DeSoto Peninsula dry most of the time, but breaks in the levee led to flooding around the camps, which made living conditions difficult for the men. (*Harper's Weekly*)

◀ By the time crews cut the dam, the canal had become effectively obsolete. (*Harper's Ferry*)

were digging the canal and fighting off the water of the Mississippi, which continued to rise and threatened to drown us."

The Confederates were of a different mind. As late as early March, Grant's enemies on the far bank were predicting the canal's successful completion. On March 7, however, the dam at the upper end of the canal gave way with "a heavy rush of water," and the Mississippi poured in. Much of the dam's infrastructure was destroyed or flooded. Over the next several days, Prime tried to use barges to block the breech and a piledriver to help with repairs. Frantic work seemed to salvage the operation. Even Grant believed success was now possible. On March 12 he wired to General Halleck, "The canal is near completion…. I will have Vicksburg this month, or fail in the attempt."

In the end, Confederate artillery proved decisive, not in its accuracy but in its capacity as a deterrent. By March 17, the dredges had worked their way to the southern end of the canal and came within range of the Rebel batteries on the far shore. "I commenced, and kept up, both day and night, at irregular intervals, a telling fire," bragged a Confederate artillerist, "and finally drove the dredge boats … away, and put a quietus to all their work…." The harassing fire made the work too dangerous. Grant authorized the removal of the dredges. "All work … has been suspended for several days …" Grant wrote Halleck. In the end, the vague phrase "several days" turned out to mean forever. Grant had other initiatives underway that demanded his attention and his manpower.

Once the canal effort had gotten underway in late January, Grant had immediately begun casting about for other options. Forty miles north of Vicksburg, a body of water known as Lake Providence offered one such tantalizing possibility. The lake could be connected via swamps and streams to create "a wide and navigable way" all the way to the Red River some 120 miles south of Vicksburg. In river miles, that equated to a roundabout 265. The route flowed from Lake Providence to Bayou Baxter, Bayou Macon, the Tensas Rover, the Black River, and then to the Red. Most of the waterways were already known to be passible to steamers of modest size,

▲ "By the aid of this canal, it is expected that we shall be able to send boats into the Gulf, by the Black, Red, and Atchafalaya rivers...." *Harper's Weekly* reported. (*Harper's Weekly*)

although the debris-clogged Bayou Baxter presented a real question mark.

On January 31, Grant sent an engineering party, accompanied by a brigade of infantry and a tinclad gunboat, to survey the route. They camped near the village of Lake Providence, which shared a name with the adjacent lake. By the end of the expedition, the crew determined that anything they did to create a through waterway would flood out the village, which residents had recently deserted when news arrived that the Yankees were coming. Otherwise, the initial report from the engineers looked favorable. "It will only be necessary to cut a few trees so as not to interfere with chimneys," the lead engineer declared in reference to the smokestacks on the steamboats. "Once in Bayou Macon we shall have a clear coast to Red River."

▶ James McPherson, a favorite of Grant's, would meet an untimely end, surprised by enemy troops at the July 1864 battle of Atlanta. (Library of Congress)

The news pleased Grant. Sherman, who seemed to like the plan more than his own waterway project, deemed it "worthy of determined prosecution."

Grant assigned the task to his young protégé, Maj. Gen. James Birdseye McPherson, commander of the XVII Corps, then still in Memphis. "[T]his bids fair to be the most practicable route for turning Vicksburg," Grant told him. He ordered McPherson to send the division of Maj. Gen. John Logan south to provide manpower for the operation.

McPherson hoped to steam forth with Logan's men by February 10, but a lack of transports delayed departure by nearly two weeks. Cold weather upriver around St. Louis froze in the necessary boats. "I am very much annoyed but see no help for it,"

McPherson told Grant. Not until the 22nd did Logan's men finally head south.

When they arrived at Lake Providence 26 hours later, the troops discovered the work party that had preceded them had already constructed a canal that would connect the Mississippi to the lake, with the exception of a levee that still held the river at bay. The project had gone much more smoothly than the canal being cut across DeSoto Point. Elsewhere, though, the task of clearing a channel looked daunting. McPherson, a trained West Point engineer, came back dispirited from an inspection. "The work of clearing it out is much greater than I was led to believe from the Engineers Report," he admitted.

Logan's division disembarked from the transports and settled in around the village. "The soldiers are encamped all along the lake and are in splendid spirits and condition," one observer noted. "Not one of them thinks of getting sick in such a place as this.... Fishing is excellent, and ducks and geese are plenty. The foraging parties come back laden with turkeys and chickens...." Men played pick-up football games and regimental bands played cheerful and patriotic tunes. The abandoned plantations around the lake provided any number of surprising luxuries, free for the taking. Josiah Moore of the 17th Illinois wrote of everything from hogs and sweet potatoes to "a rebel piano that some of the boys pressed into service." He marveled at "the finest furniture committed to the merciless soldier."

This was a far cry from the misery under which Sherman's men toiled down at DeSoto Point. McPherson's men still had to contend with the same temperamental weather. "Sprinkling is unknown in this country," groused one storm-drenched Iowan. When it rains, "it falls in sheets of water."

Along with the extra muscle, Grant also put extra engineering expertise to work on the project. Progress went fairly smoothly, if reported somewhat over-optimistically. Complications frequently arose, usually because of fluctuating water levels. In some places, the water needed to be deeper for steamboats to pass. Along other stretches, murky floodwaters hid the watercourse entirely, "making the work of clearing out the timber exceedingly slow, and rendering it impracticable to make an artificial channel," reported Grant.

By March 4, engineers were ready to cut the levee at Ashton, LA, several miles north of Lake Providence. They mined into the earthen embankment and blew a huge load of powder to create a breech. Although water gushed through several crevasses, it only slowly flooded the country between the Mississippi and Bayou Baxter. Yet, the surge of water from the river into the adjacent swamp caused the current in the bayou to flow backwards, which flooded out unsuspecting work parties downstream.

Overall, McPherson seemed pleased and predicted that Grant would soon be able to start moving troops and materials through the waterway to the Red River, circumventing Vicksburg entirely. Grant, however, expressed less enthusiasm for the project because he thought another option might pan out sooner and with more direct results. On March 5, he stripped men from McPherson and shifted them to an effort underway at a place called Yazoo Pass.

Grant had inspected part of the Lake Providence route himself and felt less sanguine about the effort than his protégé. "[T]here was scarcely a chance of this ever becoming a practicable route for moving troops through an enemy's country," he decided. Capt. Andrew Hickenlooper, the corps' chief engineer, recommended a shorter, more practical route. By breaching the levee at the town of Lake Providence, at the southern end of the lake, it would cause a more rapid rise in the lake and enable boats to more easily reach Bayou Baxter. Grant told McPherson that his diminished corps could "let the water in to see what it will do."

Everything was ready by March 16. Artillerists fired a signal that night to warn everyone about the flood to come. The next morning, to the amazement of a large crowd of curious onlookers, engineers blew the dam. The Mississippi rushed through "with such a vehemence and noise as to make one remember the falls of Niagara," claimed one witness.

It still took several days for the river to do its work and extend its flood waters enough to make the whole route navigable, but Grant hardly seemed to care. He expected a breakthrough at any moment at one of his other operations—breakthroughs that never came to pass. Grant might have turned his attention back to the Lake Providence waterway and ordered his men to finish the remaining work, but instead abandoned the effort entirely.

While fruitless as an attempt to, for instance, shuttle troops south to join Nathaniel Banks's efforts against Port Hudson, Louisiana, the Lake Providence project did pay unexpected dividends. When Grant finally succeeded in moving against Vicksburg, the flooded swamps and bayous along the waterway would do much to protect the right flank of the Federal army as it shifted along the Mississippi. Rebel raiders would find it difficult to traverse the new watery landscape and harass Grant's movement.

Grant was not the only one keeping his men busy during this time. Admiral Porter was also seeking a way to keep his men occupied. The naval officer learned about a busy river trade near the mouth of the Red River, which emptied into the Mississippi in the stretch protected by Vicksburg in the north and Port Hudson in the south. Porter hoped to disrupt that trade.

To do so, he selected 25-year-old Charles Rivers Ellet. His father, Charles Ellet, Jr., had invented the "ram fleet"—four boats with reinforced sterns designed for ramming enemy ships that had played a pivotal role in the capture of Memphis in early June 1862. The only Federal

▼ The town of Lake Providence sat next to the lake, although most of the residents had fled at the arrival of the U.S. Army. (*Harper's Weekly*)

casualty of the engagement had been, unfortunately, the senior Ellet. Porter identified the younger Ellet as a man of pluck and courage, and indeed, Charles was ready to steam into enemy territory and see what he could do.

Ellet outfitted the strongest ram available for the task: *Queen of the West*. The warship was damaged during its summer attempt to ram the *Arkansas* along the bank of the Mississippi River. The repaired boat, packed with bales of cotton as protection against artillery, was now a "cottonclad."

On the morning of February 2, the *Queen* bolted past Vicksburg's surprised gunners and headed downriver. ("[W]hether it was from love of glory or from want of judgment" that Ellet didn't wait for the cover of darkness, Porter couldn't decide.) In three days, the ram captured and burned three Confederate supply boats and returned to safe harbor on February 5, none the worse for wear. The Confederates now saw the warship as a grave threat. "The worst that has befallen this place, and perhaps the entire Confederacy, since the arrival of the Yankee army on the peninsula across the river, is the interference with our communication with Red River," worried one resident.

Porter decided to try it again. "[B]urn, sink, and destroy," he instructed Ellet, but be careful, he added. The last thing Porter wanted was to lose one of his most valuable boats.

Ellet set off again. He reached the Red River on February 14 and promptly captured another steamer. The emboldened

▲ Between Vicksburg and Port Hudson, Confederate commerce steamers still transported goods, such as these cattle, across the Mississippi. Stopping that trade became an important Federal objective. (*Harper's Weekly*)

▼ According to one witness, when the *Queen of the West* rammed the commerce steamer *Vicksburg* then passed "down the river uninjured, they were not less astonished than chagrined, because it was believed, by them at least, that no Union steamboat could safely pass their formidable batteries." (Library of Congress)

▲ Following her capture by Confederates in February 1863, the *Queen of the West* served as a Confederate ram until Federals destroyed her the following April. (*Harper's Weekly*)

Ellet decided to chug farther upriver and try his luck against a Confederate position known as Fort Taylor. The engagement was over quickly when the *Queen of the West* ran aground. The warship was now easy prey for the artillerists of the fort, who quickly disabled the ram with a single lucky shot through a steam pipe. Ellet and his crew scrambled aboard the steamer they had captured and made a getaway.

Ellet's men made it down to the Mississippi and pointed their steamer upriver. They soon came upon the ironclad *Indianola*, sent by Porter to reinforce their effort. After filling in the *Indianola*'s captain about what had happened, Ellet continued northward back to base. The ironclad, meanwhile, tried to blockade the mouth of the Red River on its own. Confederate forces in Louisiana had other ideas and eyed the gunboat as a possible prize. On February 24, they set out to capture it.

An upriver chase ensued, with several Confederate boats—including the recently captured *Queen of the West*—steaming after the powerful but slower ironclad *Indianola*, which had its coal barges lashed to either side. A 90-minute battle erupted and the *Indianola*, crippled by repeated rams from the *Queen of the West*, took on water. The captain took the boat to the Louisiana side of the river so his crew could escape. Once they were clear, he surrendered and Confederates towed the waterlogged vessel to the Mississippi side of the river just offshore of Jefferson Davis's homestead at Davis Bend. There, the *Indianola* settled to the bottom in about ten feet of water.

Rebel salvage crews went to work immediately with the hope of raising the gunboat and converting it to Confederate use. Work had only been underway for a day and a half when, on February 26, a second ironclad appeared from upriver. Frightened (and possibly a little drunk),

▼ The USS *Indianola* would have a short but infamous career. (*Harper's Weekly*)

the work crews torched the *Indianola*, burning it to the waterline rather than letting Federals recapture it.

The second ironclad turned out to be no ironclad at all. Members of the *Indianola*'s crew had made it upriver and had alerted Porter. The admiral didn't want to risk losing a third vessel, so he instead "hit upon a cheap expedient, which worked very well." He ordered the construction of a new ironclad which his men rigged together in 12 hours. It wasn't a ship at all, but a decoy made from a 300-foot raft complete with a pilot house, chimneys made from stacks of pork barrels, a casemate with fake guns protruding out of fake ports, and a U.S. flag flapping in the river breeze. An ingenious sailor had even rigged up a way for smoke

▲ The *Indianola* made its first run in full daylight in open defiance of Confederate batteries. (Naval Heritage and History Command)

◀ Federals duped Confederates into destroying the *Indianola* after its capture. Had Confederates restored the gunship, it would have posed a formidable problem for the Federals. (Naval Heritage and History Command)

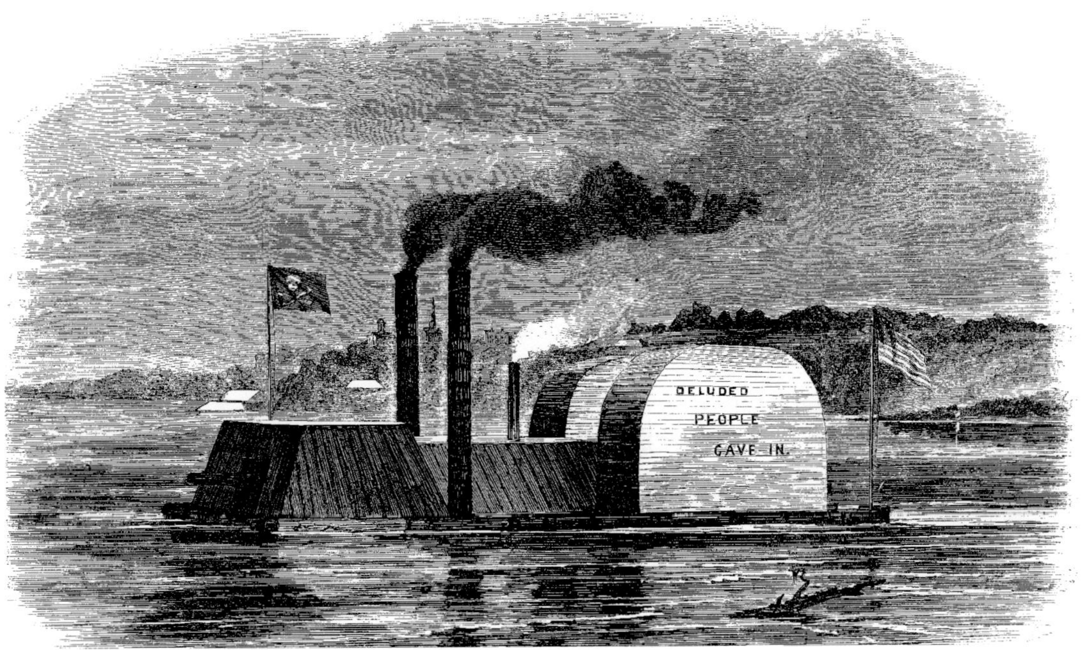

▲ The fake Federal gunboat that triggered the *Indianola*'s destruction included a bit of soldier snark. (*Harper's Weekly*)

to come out of the stacks. Crews painted the craft a drab color to make its appearance more confusing and wrote "Deluded People Cave In" on the side of its ersatz wheelhouse. The entire enterprise cost $8.23. It was money and time well spent, thought Porter, considering the grief it saved him given he no longer had to contend with a refurbished *Indianola* terrorizing his fleet.

Still, the adventure south to the Red River had cost him the ironclad and the *Queen of the West*. "My plans were well laid, only badly executed," the admiral wrote to Welles. "I can give orders, but I can not give officers good judgement." He described the episode as "the most humiliating affair that has occurred during this rebellion."

The Yazoo Pass

General Sherman's December Chickasaw Bayou expedition had tried to use the Yazoo River as an avenue to outflank Vicksburg by steaming up from the mouth of the river. In late January, Grant learned that it might be possible to use the Yazoo to approach Vicksburg from the north, upriver, through the Mississippi Delta.

Six miles below Helena, Arkansas, and on the opposite bank, a steamboat cut-off had once connected the Mississippi River to a waterway known as the Yazoo Pass. At the northernmost end of the pass was a mile-long channel connecting the Mississippi to Moon Lake, a crescent-shaped body of water that had once been an oxbow turn of the river long-since sealed off by the river's ever-changing course. About four miles down the lake's eight-mile length, the pass flowed out through a tree-obscured channel. Between 75–100 feet wide along its length, it ran from the lake 12 miles to the Coldwater River. The Coldwater,

▼ According to *Harper's Weekly*, "the Yazoo is a peculiar, dreary, unwholesome steam, its pale-green, sickly-looking waters having their originals in swamps, and being so fatal to health that it is well named ... the 'River of Death.'" (Chris Mackowski)

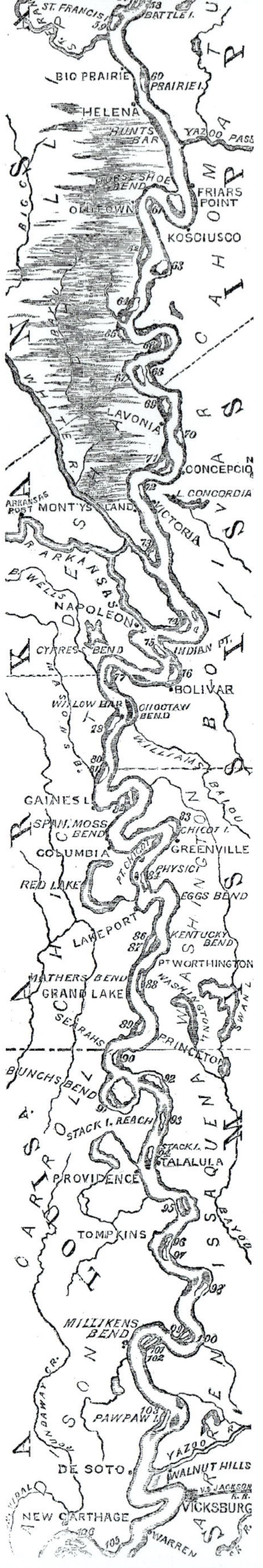

Bearss on the Delta

"Land surfaces are low and level and, prior to the construction of an extensive levee system, much of it was submerged in the late winter and early spring of the year. The Delta waterways were crooked, and so soft was the soil that the river bends were continually cutting into one another. This caused the streams to seek new channels, and left many crescent-shaped bodies of stagnant water. There were no railroads in this region and the few roads were built along the highly cultivated natural levees bounding the waterways."

— Ed Bearss, former historian, Vicksburg National Military Park

in turn, connected with the Tallahatchie River, which connected with the Yazoo.

In response to the delta's growing number of cotton farmers, the state had constructed a series of levees lining the east bank of the Mississippi, including—in 1856—an earthen dam 100 feet thick and 18 feet high built across the mouth of Yazoo Pass to seal it off.

If opened and if navigable for the Federal navy, the Yazoo Pass would allow Grant to turn the Confederate right, which was anchored on high ground at a place called Snyder's Bluff north of the Hill City. The batteries there had prevented the Federal Navy from transporting Sherman's force any farther up the Yazoo, necessitating the ill-fated landing at Chickasaw. Pemberton had since set corps commander Maj. Gen. Carter Stevenson to work strengthening the line. His 22,000 men covered the 12 miles between the bluff and the city, with good interior lines for shifting men from point to point, as needed. "Vicksburg is daily growing stronger," Pemberton reported. "We intend to hold it."

Grant saw other benefits to the Yazoo Pass route, as well. "[T]he expedition will be able to capture all the transports in the Yazoo and tributaries and destroy two gunboats said to be in course of construction," he wired Halleck. The route would also give the naval arm access to a railroad bridge up the Yalobusha River near Grenada, as well as several steamers

◀ The mouth of the Yazoo Pass is at the top right of the map; Vicksburg is at the bottom right. (*Harper's Weekly*)

▶ Along the flowing Yazoo River on December 26, 1862, troops from General William T. Sherman assembled for a march on Vicksburg through the winding roads and swamps of Chickasaw Bayou. Just two weeks earlier, the Union ironclad gunboat USS *Cairo* was sunk by a Confederate mine upriver near this location. (John Castaldo)

on the Big Sunflower River—all of which the warships could destroy.

Jefferson Davis, a former resident of the region, knew of the Yazoo Pass and worried about its potential usefulness to the Yankees. "Has anything or can anything be done to obstruct the navigation from Yazoo Pass down?" he inquired of Pemberton on January 29. In fact, shortly after taking command in Mississippi, Pemberton had ordered a reconnaissance of the area. Naval officer Isaac Brown—the Confederate hero of the ironclad *Arkansas*—gathered the intelligence himself. "[I]f the Yazoo Pass continues to remain unobstructed," he concluded, "it may, at high water, afford the enemy a passage for their gunboats into the Coldwater River, then to [Yazoo City]."

Brown tried to offer some useful recommendations. "I am not sure that permanent obstructions can at this time be placed in the pass, but if the trees along its banks were felled from both sides into the channel … they would offer serious impediments to its navigation," he reported. The trees would remain underwater a sufficient depth to stop the passage of gunboats, he believed, and the current would stir up the muddy water to make the submerged trees "invisible."

On the same day Davis wrote to Pemberton to inquire about the pass, Grant sent his chief topographical engineer, Lt. Col. James H. Wilson, on an expedition to investigate the waterway. The 26-year-old Wilson had graduated sixth in the West Point Class of 1860 and had started the war in the Eastern Theater, where he served under Maj. Gen. George B. McClellan. When he came west, he immediately impressed Grant with his trouble-shooting attitude and energy. Grant called him a member of "the get-there gang."

On January 31, Wilson set out from Helena with 500 men packed onto the tinclad *Forest Rose* and the steamers *Henderson* and *Hamilton Belle*. They soon arrived at the closed-off mouth of Yazoo Pass and, by midafternoon on February 2, crews began working on the dam.

Water in the Mississippi was eight feet higher than the water table on the canal side of the dam. Wilson directed his men to dig two ditches from the river side of the dam to the canal side. Once finished, they dug a mine and inserted 50 pounds of gunpowder. The plan was to blow a hole in the dam, with the water rushing through from the river scouring a path between the two ditches.

Wilson blew the dam on the evening of February 3. A geyser of dirt and mud sprayed into the air and the Mississippi rushed into the breech, gouging a huge channel as intended. Wilson had his men dig two additional mines to widen the 40-

▲ Isaac Newton Brown circumnavigated the globe with the U.S. Navy before resigning his commission at the outbreak of the war. He had a distinguished career with the Confederate Navy. (*Battles & Leaders of the Civil War*)

yard gap, "the water pouring through like nothing else I ever saw except Niagara Falls," Wilson reported. "Logs, trees, and great masses of earth were torn away with the greatest of ease. The work is a perfect success." By the following morning, Wilson had created a gap 75 yards wide, which was more than wide enough for naval vessels to slip through safely.

It took a few days for the Niagara rush of water to slow. Once it did, Wilson had to determine if the pass was actually passable. On February 7, George W. Brown, commander of the tinclad *Forest Rose*, entered the lake with 22 men aboard and steamed as far as the exit channel. Several large plantations lined the east side of the lake. A landing party went ashore to gather intelligence. The men talked with others who had just come up the pass from the Coldwater River and discovered that Confederates downriver "were fully apprised of the expedition before, or as soon as, the work was commenced." The Rebels were busy working to obstruct the Coldwater with felled trees.

▼ James Wilson would enjoy a successful career in the army because of his own talents and the patronage of his mentor, Grant. (Library of Congress)

Brown's men also captured a pair of Confederate partisans who claimed to have been part of the tree-chopping detail. Other partisans—members of a Mississippi cavalry unit—prowled about the countryside. Brown's men "heard sounds in the woods and took arms, but saw nothing, and we returned safely, not knowing that we had had a very narrow escape of our lives."

Engineer Wilson seems almost dismissive of the Confederate efforts because navigation had thus far been smooth and nearly problem-free. "[A]lthough many more trees may have been cut lower down, and at points opposite each other, they will not materially affect navigation," he countered with what would later prove to be overconfidence. He seemed more concerned about the overgrowth of tree branches that might knock over smokestacks.

Confederate Naval Officer Isaac Brown, for his part, seemed to concur with Wilson's assessment. "Our pass obstructions will only delay the enemy," he said on February 9 when he warned Pemberton about the Yankee presence. "The enemy have cut the Yazoo pass levee; contemplate, perhaps, assailing us down the Yazoo." Pemberton, though, did not "think the movement probable" and would not take the threat seriously until the seventeenth. That gave the Federals 10 relatively free days of work—which they would squander, as events turned out.

The work started industriously enough. About 1,000 reinforcements from Helena arrived, bolstering Wilson's work parties, all of which set about the task of clearing the channel. Equipment often proved inadequate. "I thought at first that the trees could be trimmed up and hauled out by block, tackle, and capstan," Wilson later wrote, "but I soon found that this method was too slow and that as fast as we cleared out the obstructions above, the enemy made new ones below." In the end, they resorted to the brute strength of the men. Crews tied ropes and cables to trees, some as heavy as thirty or forty tons, and then strung out "four or five hundred men with orders to lay hold and march." The plan, Wilson said, proved entirely efficacious. "The combined strength of a full regiment was irresistible…."

Exhaustion, made worse by the weather, worked on the men like a plague. "Rain was abundant," wrote one soldier. "Underfoot was mud and water, and that constantly." Rafts, or manmade obstructions, coupled with clashes with partisans, added additional troubles. The Federals, however, moved down the Yazoo Pass as inexorably as the muddy current.

Navy vessels, meanwhile, were on their way. Once Grant told Porter about the possible route, Porter mobilized his assets, sending Lt. Cmdr. Watson Smith to the pass with a small flotilla of boats consisting of three tinclads and an ironclad (the *Chillicothe*), which would later be joined by another pair of tinclads, two rams, and the ironclad *Baron de Kalb*. Grant detached 600 men from Sherman's force to act as Marines.

Porter sounded like a worried parent as he doled out orders to Smith. "Do not enter the Yazoo Cut until the current is quite slack," he warned. Until the water levels equalized, the Mississippi's flow into the pass would be too strong. Proceed carefully and only in the daytime, Porter added. Send some small transports ahead of the gunboats to "cut away the trees and branches, so as not to endanger the smokestacks and the steamers." As far as any enemy steamers, "[t]hese you will not have time to capture; therefore you will destroy them …" ordered the admiral.

▼ The USS *Chillicothe* joined the river fleet in January 1863 in time to participate in the capture of Arkansas Post. (Library of Congress)

▶ The USS *Baron DeKalb*, formerly named the USS *St. Louis*, was one of the seven original city-class ironclads for the river fleet. (Library of Congress)

"Obtain all the information you can in relation to ironclads, and destroy them if you can while they are on the stocks." He included a small laundry list of additional instructions: get two barges of coal for fuel; keep track of the value of property that falls into your hands; parole any prisoners except officers; and don't engage batteries with your lightest vessels.

"If this duty is performed as I expect it to be," Porter concluded, "we will strike a terrible blow at the enemy, who do not anticipate an attack from such a quarter. But you must guard against surprise, and if overwhelmed run your vessels on the bank and set fire to them." It was practical, if foreboding, advice.

General Pemberton awoke from his apparent stupor after a February 17 message warned him the enemy was "coming through." He shifted troops and artillery in an attempt to mount a defense somewhere along the river and authorized the evacuation of the gunboats at Yazoo City still under construction. The defensive effort fell to 44-year-old Maj. Gen. William Wing Loring, who had overseen the Confederate line along the Yalobusha River in opposition of Grant's move south from Holly Springs. Loring was an experienced veteran of the war with Mexico and left an arm there, but he was disagreeable as a subordinate. In the last winter months of early 1862, Loring had led a group of malcontented officers in an attempted coup against Maj. Gen. Thomas "Stonewall" Jackson in the Shenandoah Valley. The War Department transferred Loring to southwestern Virginia, where he kicked up another fuss about recruiting practices. Loring eventually landed under out west in Pemberton's command, where he would once again prove difficult.

The spot selected for the defense was a narrow neck of land between the Tallahatchie and Yazoo rivers, two and a half miles above the town of Greenwood. It was, claimed Loring, "the only point short of Yazoo City where any defense can be made on the river." The right bank rose eight feet above the water, providing an impromptu artillery platform where several pieces, including two large field guns, a 32-pounder rifled cannon, and a 30-pounder Parrott Rifle, were mounted. Infantry and slaves impressed for the job dug fortifications and constructed a log barricade with 600 yards of open ground in front. Cotton bales inside the fort added additional shielding. The Rebels dubbed their position "Fort Pemberton."

Confederates also scrambled to obstruct the river above the fort with a partially completed raft and sunk one of their steamers, *Star of the West*, in the middle of the channel behind the raft. The river was narrow enough that only two ships could approach at once, side by side, and only by a long straight open stretch exposed to Confederate artillery fire.

◀ Before the Civil War, William Wing Loring fought in the War for Texas Independence, the Second Seminole War, the Mexican War, and various Indian wars. After the war, he served in the Egyptian army for nine years. (*Photographic History of the Civil War*)

Wilson's expedition bogged down in front of a Confederate obstruction blocking the entrance into the Coldwater River. Crews managed to break through on February 20, and two days later steamed into the Coldwater. Meanwhile, Smith's fleet entered the upper reaches of the Yazoo Pass on February 24 and immediately pushed ahead to meet up with Wilson's expedition. It took the convoy three and a half days to cover the 12 twisting miles to the Coldwater. Banged up, the fleet took a couple days to effect repairs. On March 3, the naval force began descending the Coldwater. By the 6th they tied up 12 miles below the confluence of the Coldwater and the Tallahatchie and again took stock of their condition. The bumping and bruising against the sunken trees and other obstructions had seriously damaged many of the hulls, such that Smith worried about the structural integrity of more than one of his ships.

Grant, meanwhile, began shifting additional infantry reinforcements to the Yazoo Pass. He redirected Maj. Gen. Isaac

◀ Some of Fort Pemberton remains preserved and is listed on the National Register of Historic Places. (National Park Service/Mississippi Department of Archives and History)

▲ Following the Union defeat at Chickasaw Bayou in December 1862, General Ulysses S. Grant requested that the U.S. Navy attempt to sail down a number of different waterways to bypass Vicksburg's defenses. In February 1863, navy gunboats sailed through the Yazoo Pass and down several rivers, finally arriving northwest of Greenwood, Mississippi on March 11, 1863. The delay of their travel granted Confederate troops time to build a large fort at a critical bend of the Tallahatchie River, named Fort Pemberton. The navy gunboats found the fort too well-positioned and armed to safely pass it, nor could they disembark soldiers to cross the muddy, swampy terrain to assault the fort. After several weeks of staring down Fort Pemberton's guns, the U.S. Navy withdrew back upriver in defeat. (John Castaldo)

► From this position looking up the Tallahatchie River, U.S. Navy gunboats halted in the face of heavy Confederate cannon fire from Fort Pemberton. For several days the gunboats tried bombarding Fort Pemberton from upriver, but the Confederate guns heavily damaged the Union ironclads. The narrowness of the river prevented more gunboats from participating in the bombardment and gave little room to maneuver for the few ships that could position themselves to attack Fort Pemberton. (John Castaldo)

Star of the West

Star of the West, a side-wheel merchant steamer launched in 1852, had attracted the first hostile shots of what became the Civil War.

On January 9, 1861, *Star of the West* tried to deliver supplies to U.S. soldiers garrisoned at Fort Sumter at the mouth of Charleston harbor. South Carolina had declared its secession from the United States on December 20, 1860, and state officials considered the U.S. soldiers an occupying force. They therefore ordered students from the South Carolina Military Academy—known today as the Citadel—to open fire on the ship from an artillery battery on nearby Morris Island. The captain of the *Star of the West* felt the mission was too dangerous and turned around, and the garrison went without being resupplied.

Confederates captured the ship along the Texas coast in April 1861 and took it to New Orleans. It was a hospital ship and naval station until the fall of the city in April 1862, at which time it was sent up the Mississippi to avoid recapture. Confederates used it as a commercial transport on the river until its destruction.

▲ This sketch, based off an 1887 photograph, shows the ignoble final resting place of the once-famous *Star of the West* along the banks of the Tallahatchie River, opposite the site of Fort Pemberton. (*Battles & Leaders of the Civil War*)

▶ A math and philosophy professor before the war, Isaac Quinby would take ill by the end of the Yazoo Pass expedition, but he would return to duty later in the Vicksburg campaign. After the war, he returned to his post at the University of Rochester. (Emerging Civil War)

Quinby, destined for James McPherson's Lake Providence project, to Moon Lake. Quinby's orders were to take infantry command of Wilson's expedition, troops then under Maj. Gen. Leonard Ross of the Helena garrison. Quinby, a former math professor, arrived on March 8, anchored on the Arkansas River, and assessed the situation. The dark, flooded lake boded ill for his large troop transports. "I shall push forward my division with all possible dispatch," he wrote to Ross, "but am, of course, dependent on suitable transports."

Loring likewise used the extra time to write Pemberton for reinforcements. Pemberton, however, hesitated to send more men to him. By this point Grant's many initiatives—as frustrating and ultimately fruitless as they were turning out to be—nonetheless began paying some unexpected dividends. The various efforts created a fog of war around Vicksburg in several directions. With so many possible threats, Pemberton had no way of knowing which of them, if any, posed a significant risk to Vicksburg. As a result, he had no choice but to defend against all of them. This problem would continue to bedevil Pemberton as March turned into April, and only increase in magnitude as April turned into May.

Watson Smith made slow progress, but on March 11, shortly after 10 a.m., his fleet rounded a bend in the Tallahatchie with the ironclad *Chillicothe* prudently in the lead. Some 800 yards away, Rebel gunners in Fort Pemberton opened fire. "Give them blizzards, boys!" Loring shouted to his men. "Give them blizzards!" The cry would soon become his nom de guerre: "Old Blizzards."

The *Chillicothe* backed off under the barrage, but tried again around 4:15 p.m., supported by the *De Kalb*. Three shots hit the ironclad, denting its shield without doing any real damage. A fourth shot, however, struck one of the ship's guns as its crew was loading it. The Federal shell exploded and "ignited her shell just after it was in the muzzle of her port gun, and it not being home [pushed all the way in] exploded at or about the muzzle." The gun crew, said Smith, was "rendered perfectly useless, 3 men being killed outright, 1 mortally wounded, and 10 others seriously wounded, while the other 5 of the gun's crews had their eyes filled with powder." The *Chillicothe* backed off again.

The fleet tied off upriver and pickets lined the banks to guard the ships. Wilson ordered a reconnaissance toward the fort while foragers fanned out to hunt for supplies. "The fleet lying then on the bend of the river, with lights shining, bands playing and men scattered about, among the close and gloomy southern trees, made a grand, impressive scene," a surprised Iowan discovered upon his return from foraging.

The fleet spent March 12 fortifying, with Federals building a pair of gun emplacements on the west side of the river positioned to enfilade the fort. Otherwise, General Ross's infantry was stymied. An

A Want of Boats

While Grant's Army of the Tennessee operated on the Mississippi River, it faced a shortage of adequate boats—perhaps a perplexing idea considering the massive amount of commerce along the river. But Grant's army was competing for boats with William Rosecran's Army of the Cumberland, which was being supplied, in part, by its namesake river out of Nashville. Federal forces in southeast Missouri needed boats and Maj. Gen. John Pope in Minnesota needed boats. Maj. Gen. Horatio G. Wright, commander of the Department of the Ohio, also needed boats. "[E]verybody is complaining of me here for want of boats," said Grant's superintendent of transportation, Lewis B. Parsons.

Grant needed boats for his supply line from Memphis, but his men also needed them for protection from the Mississippi itself. Most of them encamped in low, swampy areas that could easily and quickly be inundated. "I found the river rising so rapidly that there was no telling what moment all hands might be driven to the boats," Grant told Henry Halleck.

Not all boats were created equal, either. Grant needed many small boats rather than fewer large ones because the large ones could not travel through the narrow, cramped bayous. Through February and March 1863, an elaborate swap had to be worked out among the competing parties so everyone could get the sorts of boats they needed for the specialized circumstances they faced. This was true for both the army and the navy.

Beyond that, logistics needed to be in place to support the boats. Coal steamers could not always use wood as a substitute fuel. Iron- and tin-clad boats needed replacement parts. Ammunition stocks for various naval artillery had to be procured.

This logistical puzzle was made worse by the poor work of unscrupulous private contractors. A March 26 letter to Secretary of the Navy Gideon Welles from Rear Adm. David Dixon Porter provides an example of this. Porter pinned part of the failure of the Yazoo Pass expedition on the failure of one of the ironclads to stand up to an artillery pounding. The bolts that held the gunboat's iron plating in place popped off under fire and basically turned into shrapnel. Porter wrote:

> The *Chillicothe*, from all accounts, has proved herself unfit to engage a battery, the bolts confining the iron to the ship having been found very destructive to those on board....
>
> I consider Mr. Hartt to blame for not attending to the details of these vessels, which I find very defective. I have less hesitation in saying this much from the knowledge of the past the Mr. Hartt has not attended properly to anything out here; that the vessels he fitted in a very indifferent manner, and required extensive alterations; that some mortar boats he built came to me in a leaky condition, and he did not conform to my instructions in any particular except in the model. As a private individual, I would not employ him on anything, and I sincerely believe he is not doing the Government full justice.

impassable stream called Clayton's Bayou separated the artillery position from the fort, making an infantry assault across hundreds of yards of otherwise-open terrain an impossibility. Onboard the *Chillicothe*, "thirty hours' hard labor" got the vessel ship-shape again—or as close as possible considering repairs had to be made in the middle of a dismal swamp in enemy territory.

On March 13 the flotilla tried again. *Chillicothe* and *De Kalb* traded shots with the fort throughout the day. A raft with a 13-inch mortar aboard joined them. "The rebels fired with great accuracy" reported Smith, and their shots "struck with telling effect." Meanwhile, dense smoke lingering between the trees prevented Federals from seeing how much of an effect their own shots were having. The exchange ended when darkness fell. By that time the Federals had suffered three dead and nine wounded. Confederates lost one killed and 18 wounded, 16 of whom were burned while fighting a fire started by a Federal shell that hit an artillery magazine.

Wilson, by his own admission, was "disgusted" by the effort. "Bah!" he wrote to Grant's chief of staff John Rawlins, the contempt dripping from his pen. "I have no hope of anything great, considering the course followed by the naval forces under the direction of their able and efficient Acting Rear-Admiral, Commodore, Captain, Lieutenant-Commander Smith. One chance shot will do the work; we may not make it in a thousand.... One good gunboat can do the work, and no doubt; the two here are no great shakes."

March 14–15 passed with both sides making repairs. Confederates received a major boost on the night of the fifteenth when a large naval gun arrived by transport on the Yazoo side of their fort. Federals tried bolstering their own artillery emplacement, but the fleet was starting to run low on some of their ammunition. "[T]o-morrow it is arranged to try it again, though I am not over-sanguine of success," Wilson admitted to Rawlins, "since I see a disposition on the part of the Navy to keep from a close and desperate engagement. I've talked with them all and tried to give them backbone, but they are not confident."

The Federals tried again. The ironclads made a quick dash at the fort, which

▶ Fort Pemberton sat about eight feet above the river, making it hard for Federal cannons to shoot into the fort. Mortars, thicker and shorter than traditional artillery pieces, proved far more useful at lobbing shells *into* rather than *at* the fort. (Naval Heritage and History Command)

scored several direct hits on the front of the *Chillicothe*, hermetically sealing both gun ports. Unable to fire, she backed off. The *De Kalb* followed.

A council of war convened on March 18 and determined "it is impossible, with naval forces alone, to conquer [the fort], and it being impossible for the army forces to combine in the attack in consequence of the water." Nonetheless, Quinby's reinforcements were supposed to arrive any day, so they decided to hold out. Smith, however, could not. "My health has failed under the influences of this climate until I am compelled to report myself as no longer fit for duty," he wrote to Porter. Plagued by a nervous disposition and poor health since the expedition's start—Porter later reported it to Welles as "symptoms of aberration of mind"—he had to be taken back up the Yazoo Pass. Lieutenant Commander James Foster took his place.

Soon thereafter, ominous reports began arriving about Confederate partisans still operating along the Yazoo Pass with orders to blockade the Coldwater River behind the fleet, cutting off the ships and men deep inside enemy territory. Ross and Foster decided retreat was in order after all.

While steaming upriver on March 21, the expedition ran into Quinby's long-awaited reinforcements. Quinby had finally found enough boats on March 14 to ferry most of his men into the pass, and they covered the distance in three days, with his caboose entering the Coldwater River the following day. Grant, who expressed "a great deal of confidence" in Quinby's judgment, had placed him in overall command of the Army side of the operation, and he wanted a look at Fort Pemberton for himself. He ordered the infantry to reverse direction. Foster, in command of the naval contingent, agreed and changed course back toward the fort.

Life on the Boats

"Coffee was made, 'cold-pressed,' as it was called, by turning on hot water from the engines; and when the boat stopped, or the engineer wanted to show his importance, even that could not be obtained. The meat-ration was cooked by thrusting frying pans full of it, in at the boiler-fires. About meal-times, dozens or more of men stood waiting their turns for this. Some cooked their pork by holding it on sticks over the escape pipes of the boat. At times, however, the fleet would stop, when the men went ashore to do as much cooking as might be done at once.... After a while the amazing ration of 'hard-tack and sow-belly' became almost unendurable. From so long confinement to the boats, without exercise, the digestion became impaired. Men would sit by a box of hard tack and gnaw away at it all day, and lie down tired and hungry at night. Often some poor fellow might be seen looking in at the cabin door, at dinner-time, and wishing he had been born an officer...."

— Andrew Sperry, 33rd Iowa

Quinby, too, expected additional reinforcements. He still had one brigade back at Moon Lake, and General McPherson was supposed to transfer John Logan's division over, as well. But on March 16, Grant called off the move in favor of another possible plan. "The necessity of a large force descending the Yazoo, I think, has ended by the discovery of a route in to the Yazoo from here [Young's Point] by way of Steeles bayou and other cross bayous," he said.

Grant soon gave up on both initiatives and on March 22 cancelled the Yazoo Pass expedition entirely: "I see nothing for it but to have the force return the way they went in."

Quinby knew none of this as the Federal force crept cautiously downriver once again. A "sullen silence prevails" over the land, wrote Iowan Henry Huntsman. "Truly we are in an Enemy country." That same gloom hung over the last of Quinby's men as they set out from Moon Lake to join them. "This expedition will prove a failure, I fear," thought brigade commander Col. George G. Boomer.

Old Blizzards Loring was going to do all he could to confirm Boomer's suspicions. Loring used the intervening time to lay torpedoes (mines) in the river and fortified positions around the fort's flanks. He received some reinforcements but kept asking for more. Unfortunately for him, Grant's concurrent operations along the Yazoo Pass and in Steele's Bayou made it impossible for Pemberton to decide where to best deploy his limited manpower. By March 29 Loring had 7,000 men—far more than Quinby.

Quinby was planning a flanking maneuver when time, disease, and rain conspired against him. On April 2, almost as if to invite attack, Confederate batteries fired on Federal positions. Even with the arrival of Boomer's brigade on April 3, which tipped the manpower balance back in Quinby's favor, the Federals didn't have enough men to assault with a realistic hope of success.

Grant's order to withdraw arrived on April 4, deciding the matter for everyone. "We retired in good order, which, under the circumstances, was quite surprising to me, as the enemy saluted us with a few shells at parting," reported Boomer. Not everyone was so sanguine. Infantrymen, crammed like sardines in the transports for weeks, grumbled that the whole thing was all for nothing. "[A] disgraceful and disastrous retreat—no effort made to force a passage," grumbled a Hawkeye soldier.

Confederate bushwhackers ambushed the squadron as it withdrew. Federal landing parties chased them off, then retaliated by torching nearby plantations. Nowhere, though, did Confederates make a serious effort to blockade the pass and trap the flotilla. After a tense and winding trip back, the expeditionary force reached Helena, Arkansas, on April 10. "Cramped

▶ A newspaper correspondent wrote, "The sunset scenes down the Mississippi, in spite of the dreariness of the landscape, are often splendid—gorgeous in light and shadow and variegated tints ... like a flash of imagination into an inspired soul." (*Harper's Weekly*)

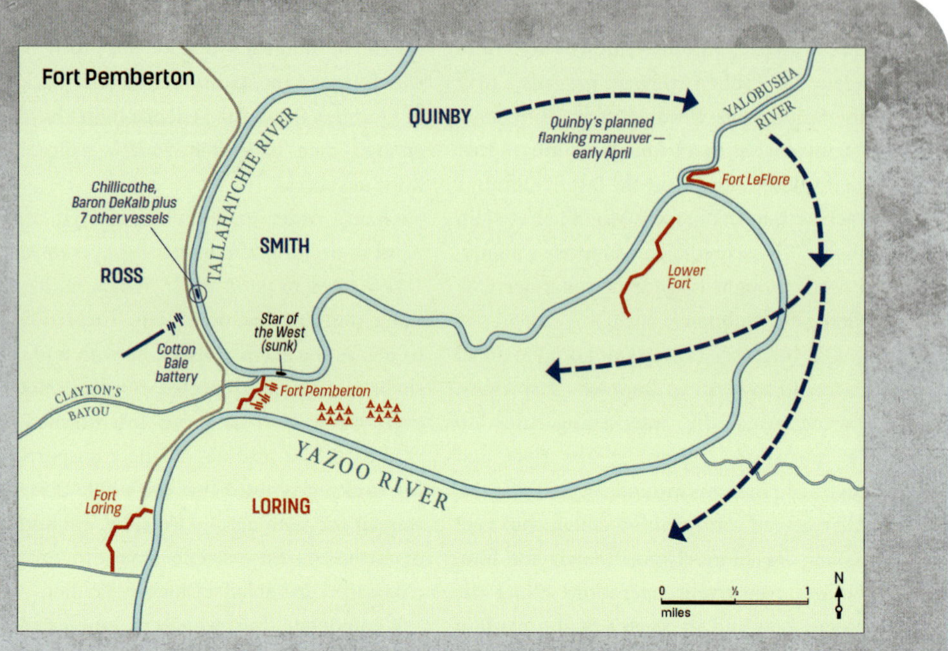

▲ A loop in the Yazoo River created a loop of land that proved an ideal location for Fort Pemberton, protected by other waterways and fortifications on its flanks and rear.

up as we had been for almost six weeks, on the narrow rivers in the swamps, it gave us a great feeling of relief, to come out again on the broad Mississippi, where there was room enough to breathe," wrote relieved Iowan Andrew Sperry.

Timing for the failed Yazoo Pass expedition had been everything. On March 13—nearly a month and a half after the energetic Wilson had first arrived—a puzzled Grant noted, "The Yazoo expedition seems to move slowly." River obstructions certainly played a role, but Smith demonstrated little sense of urgency. A vigorous push when he first entered the Coldwater would almost certainly have captured Fort Pemberton days before its completion and opened the way to the Yazoo. "We have thrown away a magnificent chance, to injure the enemy and all because of the culpable and inexcusable slowness of the Naval Commander in the first place, and his timidity and cautiousness in the Second," groused Wilson. For the "get-there gang" engineer, slowness and timidity were inexcusably galling failures.

From the Confederate perspective, a vigorous push by General Loring would have trapped the expedition in the narrow river. Vicksburg historian Edwin C. Bearss has speculated that "Loss of this force might have caused Grant to be replaced as commander of the Army of the Tennessee." Pemberton's indecisiveness also played a key role, but Loring showed little willingness to take a risk.

Grant's ongoing operations would continue to sow confusion that would increasingly cripple Pemberton, something Grant would masterfully take advantage of as the days passed.

Steele's Bayou

As Lieutenant Colonel Wilson, Brigadier General Ross, and Lieutenant Commander Smith steamed their way through the Yazoo Pass toward their initial meeting with Fort Pemberton, newspapers in Vicksburg reported on the Confederate response. Ulysses S. Grant read those papers because they provided commanders on both sides and in every theater with useful intelligence. From their pages, Grant learned that his counterpart, General Pemberton, was shifting troops up the Tallahatchie River to greet the Yazoo Pass expedition as Union forces moved downriver. The risk was obvious: Ross's men, who had not yet been reinforced by General Quinby, might find themselves cut off and captured.

The question of how to avoid this risk was answered by Steele's Bayou, a stream that emptied into the Yazoo River between Haynes Bluff and the river's mouth. During the battle of Chickasaw Bayou, Confederate sharpshooters on the north bank of the Yazoo harassed Sherman's forces to the point that he sent infantry upstream to flush them out. No one had thought of the waterway much since.

Admiral Porter, however, was pouring over his maps and recognized a possible route through Steele's Bayou to Black Bayou, Deer Creek, Rolling Fork, and on to the Big Sunflower River. If that was possible, the route offered "free navigation" into the Yazoo River 25 river miles above Haynes Bluff. Porter explored the bayou on March 14 and was pleased by his initial findings. He took Grant with him the next day to explore the route more fully. The pair traveled upstream nearly 30 miles. "It is narrow, very tortuous, and fringed with a very heavy growth of timber, but it is deep," explained a pleased Grant. "With some labor cutting the tree-tops out of the way, it will be navigable for any class of steamers."

Porter wanted to continue upriver with his small, powerful convoy, which included five ironclads, four mortar boats, and several tugs and transports. Grant would return to camp, but agreed to send along infantry support. He knew time was of the essence. "If we can get our boats in the rear of them [the Confederates] in time," he elaborated, "it will so confuse the enemy as to save Ross' force. If they do not, I shall feel restless for his fate."

Grant took a tug back to camp and began issuing orders. For help he turned to Sherman, who mobilized his men the following morning (March 16). Ahead of everyone, the XV Corps commander sent the 8th Missouri and some pioneers "with axes, saws, and all the tools necessary" as a work detail to begin the arduous job of tree-clearing. Sherman next directed Brig. Gen. David Stuart's infantry division to move up the Mississippi River to a place called Eagle Landing on the east bank. From there, Stuart's men would march one mile east and intersect with Steele's Bayou and embark on transports that would carry them to Porter. Unbeknownst to anyone, that one mile was nearly impossible to traverse because of bad roads and washed-out bridges, both of which would need to be repaired to complete the journey. It would take Stuart's men until the afternoon of March 19 to make their rendezvous with the transports on the bayou. Sherman, meanwhile, set off in a tug on the morning of March 16 to find Porter.

The tireless admiral had pushed onward, as planned. It was a slow, tedious journey. The farther upstream he went, the narrower the bayou. At times, crews had to heave the boats around the tightest of the hairpin turns with not an inch to spare. At other times, the boats had to ram giant trees that blocked the way. Porter marveled at how well the ironclads performed. "I never yet saw vessels so well adapted to knocking down trees, hauling them up by the roots, or demolishing bridges," he reported.

The squadron eventually reached Black Bayou, which one Federal described as "a narrow, crooked channel, obstructed with overhanging oaks, and filled with cypress and cotton-wood trees." A Federal soldier said the bayou definitely lived up to its name: "the water here is as black as a wicked man's heart, or my boots." Giant cottonwoods and cypress trees crowded in. When smokestacks hit the overhang, falling branches sometimes injured the men on the deck. Varmints of all kinds rained down, from wild cats to raccoons. "Rats and mice, driven from the fields by high water, had taken up their abode in the hollow trunks and rotten branches," Porter recalled. "Snakes of every kind and description had followed the rats and mice to these old arks of safety." Venomous snakes posed a particular problem.

▲ David Dixon Porter's memoir, *Incidents and Anecdotes of the Civil War*, contains a number of excellent descriptions of events around Vicksburg, but he is not always a reliable narrator because of his tendency to embellish some details and misremember others. (Library of Congress)

The fleet hove to in front of a plantation owned by J. C. Hill in Rolling Fork. The easy-flowing Big Sunflower River was only 32 twisting miles of Deer Creek away.

The 8th Missouri's work detail caught up with Porter, as did Sherman. Taking advantage of the remaining daylight, the two commanders decided to explore Deer Creek. By the time they finished, they had come to opposite conclusions. Porter believed he could continue on.

Sherman—who tended to view all of Grant's plans through a pessimistic, if dutiful, lens—wrote to his commander, "I don't think we can make a lodgment on high land by this route, on account of the difficulty of navigation." After offering a litany of cons with no pros, he concluded, "I will push the work."

The next day, Sherman went back to usher his reinforcements forward while Porter pushed on. Along the way, the admiral noticed huge piles of burning cotton, set ablaze by partisans on orders from Confederate authorities. "It was melancholy to see such fanatical destruction," Porter later wrote, "but as we abstained from anything of the kind ourselves it placed the two parties in strong contrast before the people of the country, and there were many remarks made not at all complimentary to the Confederate government."

The burning cotton was proof the Confederates had caught wind of the movement. What Porter did not know was that General Pemberton was shifting forces into The Delta to meet the new threat. The first contingent was Col. Samuel W. Ferguson's Rebel cavalry and horse artillery, who were already operating in the area. The troopers and guns began moving toward the intersection of Deer Creek and Rolling Fork. A second column under Brig. Gen. Winfield S. Featherston, who Pemberton urged to "act with energy and judgement," rendezvoused with Ferguson. A third column under Brig. Gen. Stephen Dill Lee began moving up the Yazoo.

Ferguson reached the confluence of Deer Creek and Rolling Fork on March 19 and began to obstruct the latter before moving down to start on Deer Creek. His men impressed slaves from local plantations at bayonet point to do the heavy chopping and hauling.

At the same time, Porter was converging on the same stretch of stream. Acting on intelligence from civilians along the riverbank, the admiral sent landing parties ashore in an attempt to stop the Confederate mischief. He also sent a 300-

▼ Stacks of cotton along the river, awaiting transport, were often confiscated by Federals or burned by Confederates to prevent confiscation. (*Harper's Weekly*)

man detachment with two boat howitzers to the Deer Creek/Rolling Fork confluence with instructions to hold that crucial point at all hazards. The detachment made it to the watery intersection and fortified atop an Indian mound and embankment "some 60 feet high, which commanded the whole country."

"I beg that you will shove up troops to us at once.... There is everything here the heart of a soldier could desire; everything is in abundance. Please send," Porter wrote in a note shot off to Sherman. He also said that it would take "all my men to defend the position I have.... I shall look for these re-enforcements.... Please send on troops.... We must have every soldier to hold the country or they will do it. Our difficulties increase."

The landing parties, supported by the occasional blast of gunboat artillery, made some headway against Ferguson's attempts to block the stream, and by the morning of March 20, the fleet had inched within half a mile of Rolling Fork. "We had only two or three large trees to remove," Porter wrote, "and one apparently short and easy lane of willows to work through."

◀ A native of Charleston, South Carolina, Col. Samuel W. Ferguson was among the group of officers who accepted the formal surrender of Fort Sumter in April 1861. (*Photographic History of the Civil War*)

It was at that time, however, that General Featherston arrived with his infantry. Together with Ferguson, he began a series of attacks that stymied any further Federal progress. "The woods became full of sharp-shooters, who, taking advantage of trees, stumps, and the levee, would shoot down every man that poked his nose outside the protection of their armor," reported Porter. Fatigue parties were driven back to

◀ Sharpshooters on the shore kept the sailors and soldiers on the decks of Porter's boats constantly vigilant. (Naval Heritage and History Command)

the boats, and the small detachment on the Indian mound, outgunned by Confederate artillery, had to abandon its position. "They were tumbling down as best they could," Porter observed, "the guns were tumbled down ahead of them; there was a regular stampede." Under the cover of the gunboats, they returned to the fleet.

Porter dashed off another note to Sherman to inform him of the crisis. The admiral ordered his men to smear slime from the river bottom onto the sides of the boats to make them slippery, and then shuttered what he could. He sounded "general quarters" and had his men cover the insides of all the portholes with hammocks to create entanglements. Artillerists loaded their guns with canister and grapeshot for close-quarter combat.

Porter's fears were well-founded. "We intend to take the boats to-night or early in the morning," Featherston had written the evening prior in a message that also requested reinforcements. The general thought twice about the proposed action, however, once he realized the boats sat in the middle of the stream, 10 to 12 feet from either bank and in water deeper than a man's head.

That night, Porter tried to let the boats drift downstream away from the Rolling Fork, but Confederates had felled trees across Deer Creek blocking the way. Sharpshooters made it impossible for crews to get out and clear the obstructions. "About sixty of them surrounded us," Porter recalled. "First it was like an occasional drop of rain. Then it was *pat, pat* against the iron hull all the time. The sharp-shooters," Porter added dismissively, "were not, as a rule, the brightest I have seen…."

▼ Confederate snipers shot through any open portholes, constantly harassing the sailors and soldiers inside the ironclads. (*Harper's Weekly*)

In the moment, however, Porter was surely deeply concerned about the safety of his men and boats. The Rebel sharpshooters sometimes edged to within pointblank range and fired into any open porthole that presented itself. Prudence dictated a firm strategy in case the worst should befall him, so Porter began making plans to scuttle his boats rather than let them fall into enemy hands. His men would have to cut through Confederate forces and escape over land. No one felt optimistic about their chances.

Sherman, meanwhile, had returned to the Hill plantation with Col. Giles Smith's brigade, which comprised the vanguard of Stuart's division. Porter's first note asking for reinforcements reached Sherman there on the night of March 19. Convinced Porter's fleet was essentially impervious, Sherman did not read any particular urgency in the dispatch. "I take it for granted the five iron-clad gunboats can fight anything that can be brought against them," he naively informed Grant, "and land forces are only needed to cover the ground, to enable them to clean out obstructions."

Sherman's thinking on the subject changed the next afternoon when he "heard the heavy navy-guns booming more frequently than seemed consistent with mere guerilla operations." His certainty devolved into a worry that solidified in the early morning hours of March 21. "[T]hat night I got a message from Porter, written on tissue-paper, brought me through the swamp by a negro, who had it concealed in a piece of tobacco," Sherman recalled. This was Porter's second note: "Dear Sherman: Hurry up, for Heaven's sake…"

An alarmed Sherman immediately sent all the men available at his disposal: three regiments from Giles Smith's brigade, the 6th Missouri, the rest of the 8th Missouri, and the 116th Illinois. "Report to the admiral that I would come up with every man I could raise as soon as possible," Sherman ordered Smith.

Smith's men had only tramped six miles before seeing signs that Confederates "had been very busy felling trees to obstruct the creek." They reached Porter by 4:00 p.m. "I found the fleet obstructed in front by fallen trees, in rear by a sunken coal-barge, and surrounded by a large force of rebels with an abundant supply of artillery, but wisely keeping their man force out of range of the admiral's guns," reported Smith. "Every tree and stump covered a sharp-shooter, ready to pick off any luckless Marine who showed his head above-decks, and entirely preventing the working-parties from removing obstructions."

Porter's 150 crewmen joined with Smith's 800 to fend off the Confederates long enough to clear obstructions and remove the coal barge. The new arrivals provided a land escort for the fleet, which tried to push its way out of the jam with little success. Featherston's men relentlessly harassed the blue-clad troops. By Sunday, March 22, the arrival of Confederate reinforcements further dimmed Federal prospects. "[W]e saw a large column of gray-uniformed soldiers swooping down on us from the woods," Porter recalled. "We opened mortar fire on them. They didn't mind it. On they came. They were no doubt determined to overwhelm us by numbers, and close us in.… Now would come the tug of war."

Almost as suddenly as they arrived, the Rebels fell into confusion. "[T]hey jumped behind trees, or fell into groups, and kept up a rapid fire of musketry. It looked as if they were fighting among themselves," Porter recalled. "But no! they were retreating before someone."

That "someone" was William T. Sherman, who had arrived with the four

▶ One good Smith deserves another: Col. Giles Smith's brigade led the way to reinforce Porter's stranded fleet, with Brig. Gen. Thomas Kilby Smith's brigade following up. (Library of Congress)

regiments of Brig. Gen. Kilby Smith's brigade. After sending Giles Smith ahead, Sherman had, alone, hopped into a canoe and paddled downstream to rouse the rest of the reinforcements anchored in Steele's Bayou. He loaded them onto a coal barge and had a navy tug pull them along, "crashing through the trees, carrying away pilot-house, smoke-stacks, and everything above deck...."

The night was absolutely black. When the men disembarked, they marched for two miles through canebrakes carrying lighted candles in their hands to see their way until they finally reached the cotton fields around the Hill plantation. Sherman let them rest once they found open ground, but as soon as daylight appeared they started forward again. "We could hear Porter's guns, and knew that moments were precious," Sherman remembered.

In places, the road along Deer Creek was still submerged, forcing the men to push through hip-high water. Soldiers slung their cartridge boxes over their heads and drummer boys carried their drums as high as they could. Sherman estimated his column covered 21 miles by noon.

Nearly to the fleet, Sherman's men encountered Confederate work parties equipped with axes trying to further obstruct the stream behind Porter to prevent the fleet's escape. They scattered before the Federal column, which deployed through a small plot of woods and into an open cotton field, with the fleet in plain sight besieged by Featherston's infantry and artillery. When Porter's men spotted Sherman's troops sweeping across the field, they erupted from their ironclads "cheering most vociferously."

Porter shouted instructions to his men, but "half a dozen rifle bullets came on board, and one of them struck the first lieutenant, Mr. Wells, in the head while I was talking to him and giving him an order. He fell, apparently dead, at my feet." Porter called for someone to remove the body but, he was also killed and fell atop Wells's corpse. An old quartermaster dragged a large quarter-inch iron plate along the deck and gave it to Porter. "There, sir," he said, "stand behind that; they've fired at you long enough." The crusty quartermaster was returning to his place of safety when a bullet passed through one of his hands.

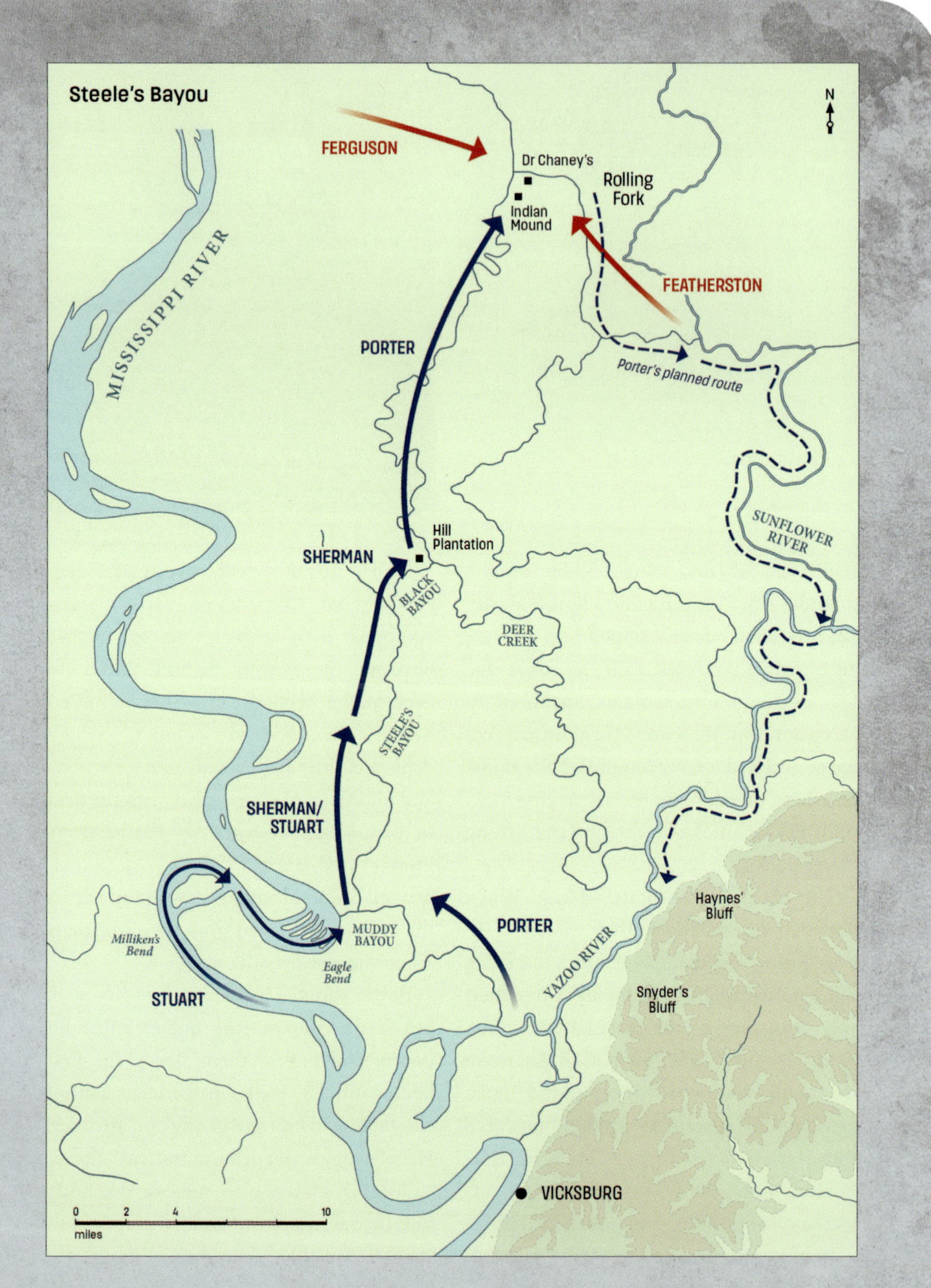

▲ Unable to get up the Yazoo River, the navy tried to go around using Steele's Bayou and approach Confederate fortifications from the north. Narrow, twisting streams allowed a relatively small Confederate force to bottleneck the expedition. Federal infantry successfully rushed to the rescue.

As Kilby Smith's men swept the field, Sherman found Porter on the deck of the gunboat using the iron plate as a shield. "I doubt if he was ever more glad to meet a friend than he was to see me," Sherman recalled.

So ended the Steele's Bayou expedition. Under cover provided by Sherman's men, it took three days to back out of Deer Creek. Confederate forces tried to converge on them, but bad weather made it impossible to do so. Sherman even dallied at the Hill plantation for a few days hoping to invite a fight, but the Rebels were unable to concentrate in enough strength. Sherman eventually withdrew.

The fleet reached the mouth of the Yazoo River by March 27, having failed in its attempt to circle past Haynes Bluff or come to the rescue of the Yazoo Pass expedition. It did, however, manage to further confuse Pemberton, who now saw threats on all sides without understanding the relative seriousness of any of them.

"It may seem ridiculous for ironclads to be wanting assistance from an army," Porter admitted, "but without that army they would likely have been in an ugly scrape."

Running the Batteries

"We get hundreds of the most ingenious and honest hints how to take Vicksburg," a frustrated William T. Sherman wrote to his brother on April 3, "but the fact is we have not yet got at Vicksburg. We have not got on shore—no man can wade the Mississippi or the deep sloughs and marshes that surround it...."

The Northern public did not understand any of that. "The cry 'On to Vicksburg' was as common as 'On to Richmond,'" reported journalist Sylvanus Cadwallader, who had become a friend and unofficial aide to Ulysses S. Grant. Although Abraham Lincoln had supported Grant's "On to Vicksburg" efforts through the early months of the year, by April 1, 1863, presidential patience was wearing thin. "[T]he President ... seems to be rather impatient about matters on the Mississippi ..." General Halleck admitted to Grant.

But by that time Grant had already mobilized his army for what would turn out to be the climactic effort of the campaign. The men who participated in the Steele's Bayou expedition were hardly back in their tents, and the Yazoo Pass expedition had not yet withdrawn from the stand-off with

▼ Sunset over Louisiana as seen from the Mississippi River near Vicksburg. (Chris Mackowski)

Fort Pemberton, when Grant sent the lead elements of his army down the west side of the Mississippi River. He had tried all he could to get at the Hill City by its northern flank, which had proven impossible. Thus far, weather, geography, and Vicksburg's batteries, had made the southern flank impossible to reach as well. But the water level of the Mississippi was falling and the land drying out, albeit slowly. "[T]he trees are now in full leaf," Sherman noted with the arrival of spring, "the black & blue birds sing sweetly and the mockingbird is frantic with joy—the Rose and violet, the beds of verbina and Mignonette ... bloom as though Grim war had not torn with violent hands" everything around them.

Now was the time to outflank Vicksburg from the south.

Sherman did not like the idea. "[T]hough it is the plan it is not a good plan," groused the general to his brother. "We commit a great mistake." Sherman preferred to go back to the drawing board. "The only true plan was the one we started with," he wrote his wife on April 10. "This Grand Army should be on the Main land, moving south along the Road [railroads] & Roads from Memphis, Holly Springs, and Corinth, concentrating on Grenada ... and then on to Vicksburg. The Gunboats and a smaller army," he continued, "should be here [on the Mississippi], and on the first sign of the presence of the main force inland, we should attack here violently."

Admiral Porter had echoed the same sentiment in a confidential note to the secretary of the navy immediately following the Steele's Bayou failure. "Had General Grant not turned back when on the way to Grenada," wrote Porter to Gideon Welles, "he would have been in Vicksburg before this."

Looking back after the war, Grant admitted to Sherman "that had we possessed in December, 1862, the experience of marching and maintaining armies without a regular base, which we afterward acquired, [Grant] would have gone on from Oxford as first contemplated, and would not have turned back because of the destruction of his depot at Holly Springs by Van Dorn." The armies that would eventually learn how to supply themselves in the interior of Mississippi, during the Overland Campaign in Virginia, and on the southern push to Atlanta and then southeast on the March to the Sea and then north through the Carolinas, did not exist in December 1862—nor did their commanders. That experience would only come through hard experience.

On March 29, Grant ordered General McClernand to march his XIII Corps to New Carthage, Louisiana, the midway point between Vicksburg and Grand Gulf on the opposite (east) bank. McClernand might have seemed an odd choice, considering his strained relationship with Grant, but the XIII Corps commander had dutifully carried out his orders all spring and expressed open enthusiasm for Grant's newest flanking plan. He was also a fighter. On the other hand, Sherman and McPherson, Grant's most trusted subordinates, were openly skeptical (and Sherman, privately hostile). Sherman went so far as to outline his long list of objections in a memo to Grant before concluding it with his typical loyalty: "Whatever plan of action [you] may adopt it will receive from me the same zealous co-operation and energetic support as though conceived by myself." Grant responded by moving ahead with his plan regardless of their opposition. "No progress was being made in any other field, and we had to go on," he explained matter-of-factly.

Sherman's negativity in no way offended Grant. "I did not regard ... the conversation

◀ The only plantation home to survive the Civil War in the area. Union troops under General Ulysses S. Grant marched past this fine plantation on their way south through Louisiana in April 1863 to start the Vicksburg Campaign. The building was often used as a headquarters for Union officers, which is why it was spared from destruction. The home's owner, Robert Moore Scott, was away fighting in Virginia with the 8th Louisiana Infantry at the time. (John Castaldo)

between us or the letter … as protests, but simply friendly advice which the relations between us fully justified," he later insisted. "Sherman gave the same energy to make the campaign a success that he would or could have done if it had been ordered by himself." Such was the strength of their partnership.

McClernand got his men underway on March 31, marching along muddy Louisiana roads and crossing unbridged streams. "The heavy artillery wheels cut through the slime and the mud, making the path a perfect mortar bed through which we waded knee deep, and where the hubs of the wheels often disappeared out of sight," one soldier recounted. A battalion of Louisiana cavalry offered token resistance, but could do little against such overwhelming numbers. On April 6, McClernand's lead division made it to New Carthage only to find the entire town underwater except for its rooftops. The men slogged onward down the river to find high ground on which to camp.

To disguise the true nature of what he was up to, Grant ordered Maj. Gen. Frederick Steele's First Division of Sherman's corps to move north of Vicksburg to Greenville, Mississippi. Steele was "to use every means to weaken the enemy by destroying their

▼ Marching down the Louisiana bank of the Mississippi River posed problems, including high water, flooded roads, primordial vegetation, venomous snakes, and alligators. (*Harper's Weekly*)

▶ On April 21, 1863, General Grant's Union troops found themselves near Dunbar's Plantation while marching south through Louisiana to cross the Mississippi River. The surrounding countryside, including the road they intended to travel on, lay flooded under several feet of water. Brigadier General Alvin P. Hovey gathered his troops and began construction of a new road and three bridges to bypass the high water. After several days of grueling work in deep water and wilderness, Grant's army was on the move again. (John Castaldo)

means of cultivating their field[s], and in every other way possible." Steele, "a small and well-knit man" with "a gentlemanly sort of repose," nonetheless had a talent for thorough destruction. This was not just the release of the winter's pent-up frustrations but a harder hand of war in general, as ordered by the War Department.

The new way of war manifested itself in other ways. Major General Lorenzo Thomas, sent from Washington to help sort out paymaster issues troubling Grant's army, began enlisting, organizing, and drilling Black troops on the Louisiana side of the river. Thousands of self-emancipated slaves had flocked to the army during its various expeditions, and while Grant initially struggled with what to do with them, Thomas seemed to find a new calling and threw himself into the task with zeal.

Already confused by the concurrent bayou operations, Steele's violent

◀ A career Army officer, Frederick Steele proved himself versatile and dependable. Following the Vicksburg campaign, he would be charged with recapturing Arkansas—which he successfully accomplished. (Library of Congress)

◀ On April 16, Grant assigned Brig. Gen. John P. Hawkins to "the command and organization of all troops of African descent in this department...." Hawkins took over work begun by Adjutant General Lorenzo Thomas. (*Harper's Weekly*)

appearance 70 miles to the north in Greenville confused John C. Pemberton. A pair of significant Union cavalry raids—plus several other smaller operations—would thoroughly muddle whatever understanding he had of what was taking place.

The first raid moved no faster than a donkey's canter. Under the command of Col. Abel D. Streight, a column of mule-mounted cavalry from the Tennessee-based Army of the Cumberland raided the Western & Atlantic Railroad between Atlanta and Chattanooga. The expedition drew Confederate forces out of northeast Mississippi in pursuit. Confederate cavalry wizard Nathan Bedford Forrest also went after the raiders, which left he and troopers unavailable to help counter the next Federal move.

The second, and much more audacious raid, was led by Col. Benjamin H. Grierson. The officer and 1,700 mounted men left La Grange, Tennessee, on April 17. If all went according to plan, the column would wreak havoc and destruction down the entire center of the state of Mississippi from north to south before either linking up with Grant's invading forces on the east bank or finding refuge in Baton Rouge.

Grierson's Raid

The sound of horses' hooves was music to Ben Grierson's ears. A music teacher at the outbreak of the Civil War, Grierson volunteered as an aide-de-camp but then enlisted in the 6th Illinois Cavalry. This was especially ironic because Grierson had nearly been killed by a kicking horse when he was eight and had a strong aversion to them.

By April 1862, in the wake of the battle of Shiloh, he earned promotion to colonel. His regiment worked to guard the flanks of the army on its advance to Corinth, and like the rest of the Army of Tennessee's cavalry, spent time harassing Confederate railroads and infrastructure. By November, he earned promotion to brigade commander. Following Earl Van Dorn's raid on Grant's supply base at Holly Spring's, Grierson pursued, forcing Van Dorn to give up on additional mayhem.

He made his biggest impact of the war during April and early May 1863. On April 17, he left LaGrange, Tennessee, with the 6th and 7th Illinois cavalry and the 2nd Iowa cavalry—1,700 men in all—on a raid through Mississippi's interior. Grierson's orders from Grant charge the raiders with "destroying all telegraph wires, burning provisions, and doing all mischief possible."

Grierson cut a path between the parallel Mobile & Ohio Railroad and the Mississippi Central Railroad, thus posing a threat to both. His troopers destroyed nearly 60 miles of track along the way and destroyed several locomotives. They torched bridges and Confederate storehouses and sowed chaos and confusion.

John Pemberton had few Confederates troopers to spare in pursuit, further stretching his resources and attention.

On May 2, Grierson arrived at the Federal garrison in Baton Rouge, Louisiana. During his 17-day, 600-mile mission, he suffered three men killed and seven wounded, and nine men went missing. In turn, he killed and wounded 100 Confederates and captured 500. Replenishing their mounts along the way, his troopers captured some 1,000 horses and mules. Ulysses S. Grant later said Grierson's Raid had "taken the heart out of Mississippi." William T. Sherman described the raid as "the most brilliant expedition of the war."

Nearly a hundred years later, Grierson's Raid became the subject of the John Wayne movie *The Horse Soldiers*.

▶ Benjamin Grierson was born on July 8, 1826, in Allegheny, Pennsylvania (now part of Pittsburgh). Four of his seven children with wife Alice survived to adulthood. He died August 31, 1911, in Omena, Michigan and is buried in Jacksonville East Cemetery in Morgan County, Illinois. (Library of Congress)

Grierson's troopers rode more than 600 miles in 16 days, destroying infrastructure, disrupting communication, sewing chaos, and evading capture at a cost of just 37 casualties. As historians William Shea and Terrence J. Winschel pointed out, the raid left General Pemberton completely bamboozled: "For the better part of two weeks, while the main body of the Army of the Tennessee was on the move across his front, Pemberton focused his attention on a few regiments of Federal cavalry in his rear."

As Grant's camps emptied on the west bank, intelligence arrived at Pemberton's headquarters about a massing of troops downriver. Pemberton dismissed the reports: "Much doubt it." He attributed the less-populated Federal camps to an exodus of transports spotted steaming upriver. "I think most of Grant's forces are being withdrawn to Memphis," Pemberton optimistically concluded. Grant was merely returning some of the boats he'd borrowed for the bayou expeditions, which he no longer needed but which other parts of the Union army did require.

The fog of war hung heavy over the Mississippi Delta in these weeks, and the Hill City was not so high as to stand above that fog for a clear view—not that Pemberton was even at his most strategically important point. The general spent most of his time toiling under piles of paperwork at the state capital in Jackson. "Enemy is constantly in motion in all directions," an exasperated Pemberton telegraphed Richmond.

Grant took advantage of the fog and confusion by informing his superiors in Washington of what he planned to do. But he did so on April 4—well after he had set his plan in motion and it was too late to stop. "This is the only move I now see as

▼ The rams USS *Switzerland* (right) and USS *Lancaster* ran the Confederate batteries on March 25, 1863. The *Lancaster* did not make it, but the *Switzerland* joined Farragut's blockade operations along the corridor between Vicksburg and Port Hudson. (*Harper's Weekly*)

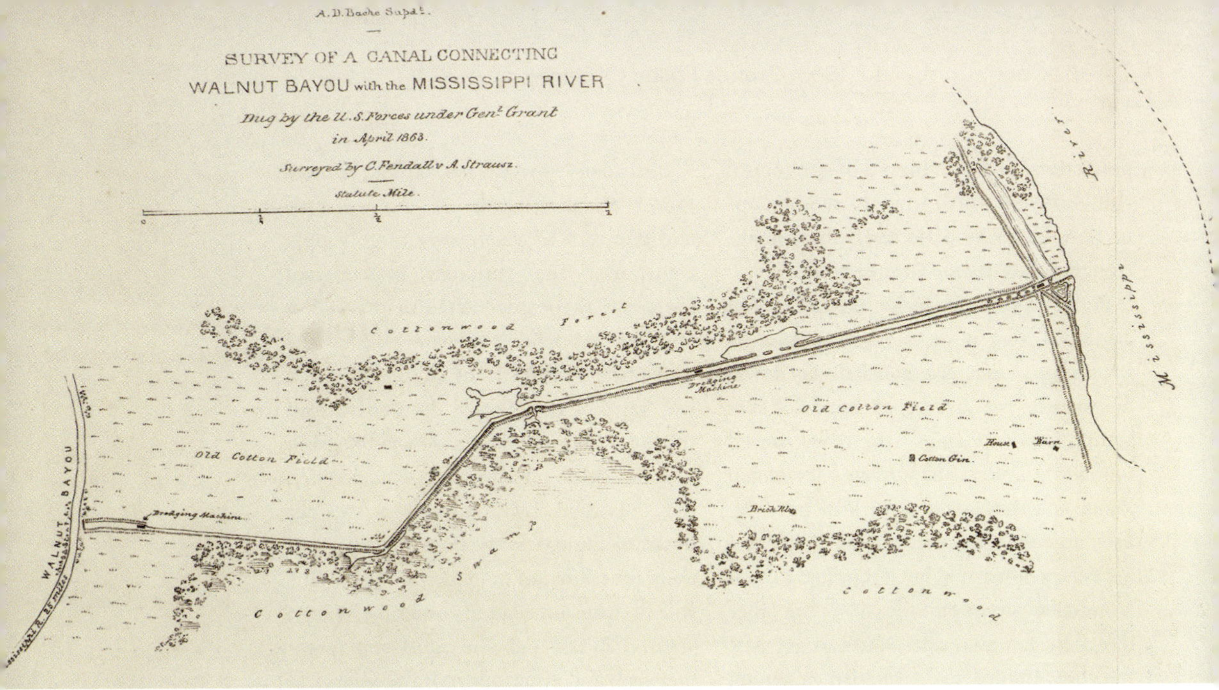

A. D. Bache Supdt.

SURVEY OF A CANAL CONNECTING
WALNUT BAYOU with the MISSISSIPPI RIVER
Dug by the U. S. Forces under Genl. Grant
in April 1863.
Surveyed by C. Fendall & A. Strausz.
Statute Mile.

▲ The Duckport Canal would breach the levee by the Mississippi, run through two and a half miles of cotton fields, and connect to Walnut Bayou. (U.S. Army Corps of Engineers)

practicable, and I hope it will meet your approval," Grant wrote.

Even as McClernand's men marched, Grant knew they would need supplies but that the muddy roads were not yet able to handle all the necessary travel. He sought yet another water route through the bayous in a solution that called for yet another canal. This one would start in Duckport, Louisiana, midway between the Federal encampments at Young's Point and Milliken's Bend. A half-mile canal would connect the Mississippi to a bayou system that linked up to Walnut Bayou three miles farther inland. The waterways meandered 37 miles to New Carthage.

A crew cut the levee on April 13 and water and boats flowed in. The channel, grumbled an increasingly cranky Sherman, was "a narrow crooked bayou with plenty of water now, but in two months will dry up." In that instance Sherman was right: the canal was not a long-term solution as a supply line. Meanwhile, "The road used is pure alluvium, and three hours Rain will make it a quagmire over which a wagon could no more pass than in the channel of the Mississippi." Too little water, or too much, and Sherman was convinced the whole scheme was doomed.

Mother Nature validated his judgment. The Mississippi water level continued dropping, and the bayous became too low for dependable travel. Grant needed a better and more reliable way to supply his men—particularly because he planned to shift McPherson southward next, with Sherman to eventually follow. He boldly decided to run supplies straight down the river on several barges past Vicksburg's big guns, and asked Admiral Porter if the navy could send a couple ironclads with them as

▶ After finding it unsafe to work on the DeSoto Canal, the steam dredges found work trying to dig the Duckport Canal instead. (*Harper's Weekly*)

protection. "Without the aid of gunboats it will hardly be worth while to send troops to New Carthage or to open the passage from here [to] there," Grant observed.

Porter agreed to make the effort but cautioned that such a move would be irrevocable. Once the ironclads go down, he warned, "we give up all hopes of ever getting them up again." The boats moved too slowly against the current, about two knots, and thus could make little headway back upriver. They could scoot quickly past Vicksburg downriver, but if they had to turn around and steam past the city in the other direction, it would take hours to get past the guns. Confederate artillerists, manning 37 heavy artillery pieces and 13 field guns, would have more than enough time to target the slow-moving vessels and sink them.

Porter had reason to steam south anyway. Adm. David Farragut had returned to the Mississippi and with only two vessels was patrolling the waters between Vicksburg and Port Hudson in an attempt to curtail Confederate river commerce. Farragut longed to return to the sea, if only Porter could relieve him of the tiresome task. Secretary Welles encouraged Porter to go.

Instead of two ironclads, as first planned, Porter assigned seven of the warships and one ram to accompany three supply transports. The gunboats lashed coal barges to their sides as extra protection and for fuel, while the army padded the transports with stacks of cotton bales and wet bales of hay. Porter decided to lead the flotilla himself on his ironclad flagship *Benton*. Grant, meanwhile, would watch the operation from aboard a steamer north of the city with his wife, Julia, and their four kids accompanying him. "This will all come out right in good time," Grant assured Julia, "and you must not forget that each and every one of my soldiers has a mother, wife, or sweetheart, whose lives are as dear to them as mine is to you."

Night was settling over Vicksburg on April 16 as Confederate officers gathered for a large party. Reports of movements on the far shore had been filtering in all day, but thus far none had amounted to much. Everyone enjoyed the festive air. On the far bank, up beyond the tip of the DeSoto Peninsula, Porter hoped the "sounds of revelry" would favor them by masking their approach.

◄ As the fleet passed beyond the range of the Confederate batteries, Federal infantry met them in rowboats, ready to pick up any men in the water. (Naval Heritage and History Command)

▲ "We have had thousands of men working by night," Sherman wrote his brother, "putting batteries as close up to Vicksburg as possible *secretly*, and in opening a channel by which we may in high water reach the River 25 miles below Vicksburg. Secrecy was essential, but the papers of Memphis announce the whole fact." (*Harper's Weekly*)

"At the appointed hour we started down the Mississippi as quietly as possible, drifting with the current," the admiral recounted. "Dogs and crowing hens were left behind, and every precaution taken to prevent the enemy from becoming aware of our design." Porter surveyed the strange flotilla, its lights extinguished to preserve secrecy. "As I looked back at the long line I could compare them only to so many phantom vessels," he recalled. "Not a light was to be seen nor a sound heard throughout the fleet."

To the men on the boats, it initially seemed as if they might somehow slip by in the dark of night unmolested. That hope ended suddenly when signal fires erupted on both banks, illuminating the river and silhouetting the vessels. In some cases, entire abandoned houses went up, torched by vigilant watch-keepers to provide as much illumination as possible so Confederate gunners could see their targets on the open river. Despite the light, an astonishing six minutes elapsed before the Rebel batteries opened fire. The artillery officers were at the ball when Porter and his fleet began slipping past; with the stations unmanned, no one was present to direct the bombardment. This mistake gave the fleet invaluable time to steam farther downriver in safety.

When the batteries finally opened, they did so with nightmarish ferocity. "[S]uch fire!" exclaimed Lt. Elias Smith of the USS *Lafayette*. "Earthquakes, thunder and volcanoes, hailstones and coals of fire; New York conflagrations and Fourth of July pyrotechnics—they were nothing to it." Smith tried to sneak a peek at the Confederate artillery, which "flashed like a thunder-storm along the river as far as the eye could see, but the incessant splatter of rifle balls, the spray from falling shot, the thunder of steel-pointed projectiles upon our sides, did not incline one to take a very protracted view of the scenery."

Porter, sliding downriver aboard the *Benton*, later feigned unconcern about "the shot rattling against her sides like hail, but she had four inches of iron plating over forty inches of oak, so that not much impression was made upon her hull. There being no longer any concealment possible," he added, "we stood to our guns and returned the enemy's fire." Porter reported that he went topside to watch the effect of his return fire. "The sight was a grand one, and I stood on deck admiring it, while the captain fought his vessel and the pilot steered her through fire and smoke…."

The ironclads ran closer to the east bank than the west in order to provide cover for the transports by absorbing as much of the Confederate fire as possible. The proximity offered an unexpected benefit: the shore batteries could not depress their guns enough to fire down at some of the gunboats. That proximity, however, came with an extra hazard. "We suffered most from the musketry fire," admitted Porter. "The soldiers lined the levee and fired into our port-holes, wounding our men, for we were not more than twenty yards from the shore." Porter claimed he was in the open atop the *Benton* at this time and thus unnecessarily exposed to the small arms fire, which casts some doubt on the accuracy of his account.

The Federal gunboats had an answer for the Confederate infantry. "As fast as our vessels came within range of the forts they opened their broadsides," Porter bragged, "and soon put a stop to any revelry that might be going on in Vicksburg."

Porter's post-action braggadocio notwithstanding, his flotilla did encounter some troubles. One ironclad, the *Lafayette*, went aground directly in front of a Confederate battery, which blasted her with nine point-blank shots before she got herself back underway. The transport *Henry Clay* was not so lucky. Enemy shells set her on fire. 'The courageous pilot … stood at his post and, with his vessel all ablaze, attempted to run past the fleet," Porter recounted. "[T]he enemy found her a good target, and showered all their attention on her." Packed with cotton bales for added protection, the blazing bales

▼ Porter used the iron hulls of his gunboats to shield more vulnerable boats as the fleet ran the gauntlet. (Library of Congress)

▲ The USS *Lafayette* joined the fleet from upriver just in time for the dash past the batteries. (*Harper's Weekly*)

were knocked overboard by the Rebel shots. "The river was covered with bits of burning cotton, looking like a thousand lamps," recalled an eyewitness. The transport soon was lost.

It took a full hour for the fleet to pass from Vicksburg down beyond Warrenton. "The air was full of sulphurous smoke," wrote Julia Grant, who observed the action alongside her husband from the deck of the *Henry Von Phul* anchored north along the Louisiana shore above Vicksburg. The site, thought another observer, "might have answered for a picture of the infernal regions." Eventually, once the last vessel was clear, "all was silent … and the river had returned to its former obscurity."

"The smoke cleared away," wrote Julia, "the stars looked down tenderly upon Union and Rebel alike, and the katydids and the frogs began again their summer songs."

▶ Confederate engineer Col. Samuel Lockett sketched the action as seen from the heights of Vicksburg. His sketch served as the basis for this image. (*Battles & Leaders of the Civil War*)

An anxious Sherman waited for the fleet below the city on the Louisiana shore. He'd ordered some of his infantry to manhandle four yawls across the swamp so they could pick up any men from damaged vessels who might float by. Sherman climbed into one and went out into the river to watch the action. "[T]he scene was truly sublime," he said. His boat rowed to meet Porter as the *Benton* steamed into view. The general hopped aboard for a quick interview, then jumped back into the yawl almost as quickly so that, like a worried parent, he could check on the other boats as they reached safety.

Sherman's crews picked up the men of the *Henry Clay*. Except for the lost transport, the running of the batteries cost the Federals only a dozen soldiers wounded. "All praise to the Lord and Admiral Porter," declared Lt. Elias Smith.

The paltry losses and ease with which they passed the vaunted batteries left Porter less than impressed: "[T]he enemy's artillery fire was not much to boast of, considering that they had over a hundred guns firing at us as we drifted down stream in such close order that it would seem to have been impossible to miss us." As far as the veteran admiral was concerned, it was all in a night's work.

Pemberton, of course, was far less sanguine. On April 17 he wired the grim news to Jefferson Davis: "I regard navigation of the Mississippi River as shut out from us now. No more supplies can be gotten from the Trans-Mississippi Department." For a government whose armies relied on those crucial supplies, Porter's feat was a devastating blow. Already held in suspicion by many in Mississippi, Pemberton came under renewed attack from within. "The people with this dept., soldiers and citizens," wrote a group of newspaper editors to President Davis, "do not repose that confidence in the capacity and loyalty of Genl. Pemberton, which is so important at this junction, whether

▼ Porter's flagship, the *Benton*, was the first to finish the gauntlet. (*Battles & Leaders of the Civil War*)

▲ The Mississippi River below Vicksburg. On the night of April 16, in a fiery display, seven of Admiral Porter's ironclads accompanied by three unmanned army transports battled their way past the city's powerful batteries and raced to a rendezvous with Grant's infantrymen south of Vicksburg. The daring passage provided Grant with the necessary means of hurling his army across the mighty river and onto Mississippi soil to begin the inland campaign that led to Vicksburg. (John Castaldo)

justly or not.... Send us a man we can trust," they implored.

Grant, meanwhile, was in high feather. On April 18, he rode down to New Carthage, which was still unusable because of the high water. He and McClernand quickly found more acceptable accommodations for the troops at a landing called Hard Times, opposite the ghost village of Grand Gulf and burned out by General Williams the previous summer. The Big Black River flowed into the Mississippi there, and it might make the perfect spot to land the Federal infantry on the east bank below Vicksburg.

Grant sent word for McPherson to begin marching south. In the meantime, in order to keep Pemberton off balance, Sherman moved up the Yazoo to demonstrate against Chickasaw Bayou. Although haunted by his previous experience there,

▶ When the fleet ran the batteries on April 16, the navy led the way. When Grant repeated the feat on April 22, it was an all-army affair. (Naval Heritage and History Command)

▲ The tug *Rumsey* took a turn running the batteries on April 26, 1863. Note the stacks of cotton on her port side, which faced Vicksburg's batteries. (Naval Heritage and History Command)

he understood the necessity for pulling Pemberton's forces north so they could not concentrate against Grant's planned river crossing below the city. Sherman's men would also protect the supply hub at Milliken's Bend until Lorenzo Thomas's new units made up of Black men could take over the task. One wonders whether Grant also kept Sherman behind in order to score some success on the east bank as a

◄ Considered the grandest plantation in the area, Franklin Plantation was owned by Dr. Allen Thomas Bowie. Franklin Planation survived the passage of the XIII and XVII Corps, but Sherman's XV Corps burned it on May 6, 1863, before anything could be salavaged. (John Castaldo)

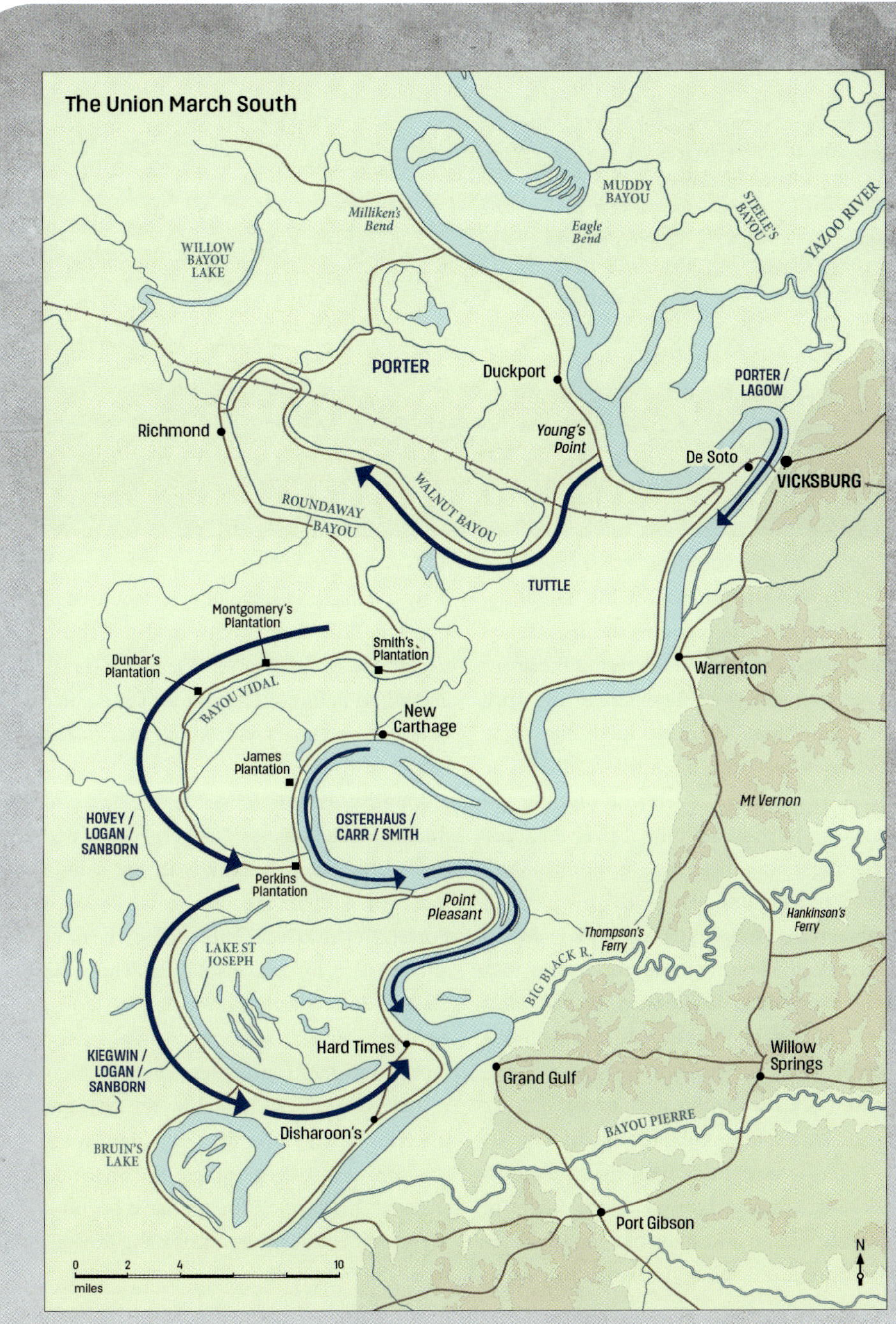

▲ Sherman's corps stay in place to guard supplies and demonstrate against Vicksburg from the north while McClernand's corps marched south, followed by McPherson's. First eyeing Hard Times plantation, they would move to Disharoon's to cross the river.

◀ Lake St. Joseph was the name of a small ox-bow lake formed from the Mississippi River. In 1863, a small but thriving community inhabited the area, dominated by fifteen stately plantation homes surrounding expansive cotton fields. On April 25, 1863, Grant's Army marched through the area on its way to Hard Times Landing. Impressed with the Union sympathies of the Nutt family at Winter Quarters Plantation, U.S. military leaders left official letters in the care of the family to protect the home. After General William T. Sherman reached the area on May 6, Winter Quarters would be the last plantation house still standing along Lake St. Joseph. (John Castaldo)

measure of reassurance for his "Doubting Billy" before bringing him south and then across the river to join the rest of the army.

Encouraged by the success of April 16, Grant and Porter decided to run the batteries yet again on April 22, this time with six transports laden with supplies and towing along an additional twelve barges. The night was "black as a bottomless pit," but Confederates were ready this time. "It seemed as though Heaven and Hell had turned everything loose to destroy us," said a man in the lead transport. The "most magnificent display of fireworks" lit the night so brightly that "a newspaper could have been read with ease" from the decks of the boats, reported one Federal.

The *Tigress*, which had once served as Grant's command vessel at the battle of Shiloh, was hit and sunk, but five of the six transports and half of the barges made it to New Carthage. Human losses amounted to two men killed and six wounded. "Thus," declared a proud Porter, "General Grant's army had below Vicksburg an abundance of stores, and boats with which to cross the river."

Months of frustration and delay had finally yielded success. "General Grant had turned the enemy's flank with his army, I had turned it with the gun-boats," declared Porter. "[N]ow Grant had to cross the river and trust to his brave soldiers, who were glad to do anything rather than sit down day after day with nothing to do but carry on the ordinary routine of an army."

They might now be below the city, but the men in the ranks knew the hard work was only just beginning. As Sherman wrote to his wife, "Here we have begun a move that is one of the most dangerous in War...."

Conclusion

Poised now below Vicksburg, Grant determined to cross McClernand's and McPherson's infantry corps to the Mississippi side of the river in the early morning hours of April 30. The Herculean task would take almost 24 hours and be the largest amphibious landing in U.S. Army history until D-Day in World War II. "I was now in the enemy's country, with a vast river and the stronghold of Vicksburg between me and my base of supplies," Grant later wrote. "But I was on dry ground on the same side of the river with the enemy."

From that point Grant's army would fight a series of battles that would carry him to the gates of Vicksburg: May 1 at Port Gibson, May 12 at Raymond, May 14 at Jackson, May 16 at Champion Hill, and May 17 at the Big Black River. On May 19 and again on May 22, he would launch attacks against Vicksburg's formidable fortifications and be repulsed with heavy losses both times. Thus chastised, Grant would do again what he had done during the first four months of the year: patiently try one plan, and then another, to try and crack the nut.

By that point, time was on his side. Pemberton's army was hemmed in from the land side, and the Federal navy secured the river side. The Confederate garrison and the citizens of Vicksburg slowly ran out of everything. Food dwindled dangerously low. Horses and dogs disappeared. Civilians moved into caves to avoid the constant shelling.

As the Confederates grew weaker Grant's command increased in both men and materiel. The arrival in his rear of the

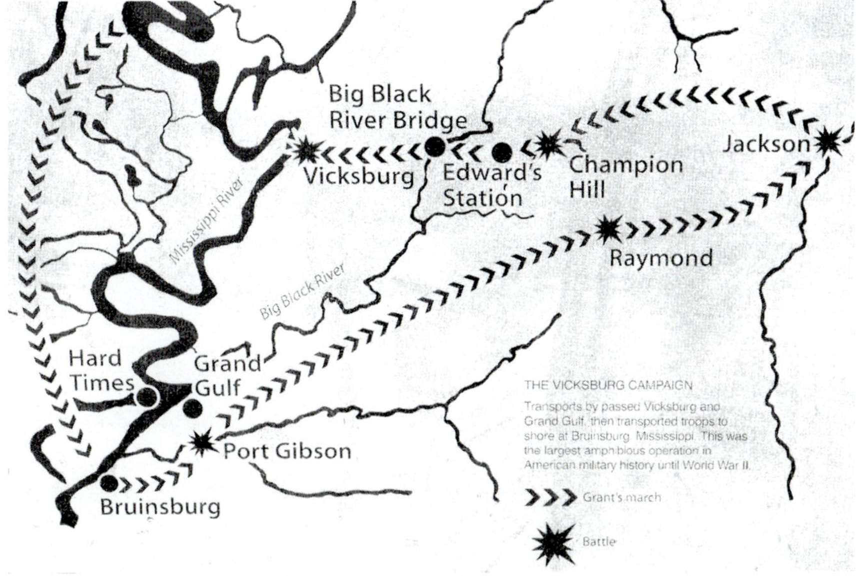

▶ Once across the river, Grant moved inland to invest Vicksburg from the east, as illustrated on a map on a National Park Service monument in Raymond, Mississippi. (Chris Mackowski)

Confederate Western Theater Commander Gen. Joseph E. Johnston and his "Army of Relief" posed a new threat when it began coalescing at Jackson. As Grant soon discovered, however, Johnston would play the part of a threatening specter lurking in the background, and little else.

Out of options, Pemberton surrendered Vicksburg on July 4, 1863.

Grant was glad to put the frustrating, waterlogged start of the year behind him. "This long, dreary and, for heavy and continuous rains and high water, unprecedented winter was one of great hardship to all engaged about Vicksburg," he reflected. Porter, whose cooperation proved invaluable to Grant, characterized those months as "a series of patient labors, more wearing than active excitement in the field; and while the enemy, on the one hand, displayed the greatest endurance and determination, we, on the other, exhibited the greatest patience under many disappointments."

Grant would later claim—matter-of-factly, if a little dubiously—that he had known all along that the only way to get at Vicksburg would be by land. "I … never felt great confidence that any of the experiments resorted to would prove successful," he claimed. "Nevertheless, I was always prepared to take advantage of them in case they did." He was really just biding his time, he explained, until he could execute his real plan, which he'd had in mind "the whole winter"—he just "did not … communicate [it], even to an officer of my staff … until the waters began to recede." Indeed, no contemporaneous account mentions a word of Grant conspiring to cross the river below the city and then make a landward attempt, although that may be because Grant had not yet developed the plan, rather than because he had not shared it.

A retrospective view of these events makes them look more inevitable, and as Grant wrote his account of Vicksburg, he was trying to preserve his legacy as a war hero and president even as he faced financial ruin and public embarrassment because a business partner had swindled him as he fought terminal throat cancer. No wonder he put the shiniest glean possible on what was arguably one of his most miserable periods of the war, and one during which public sentiment began to grow vocally restless against him.

However, such a spin sells short the invaluable lessons Grant learned during

► The Father of Waters flows unvexed. (Chris Mackowski)

▼ In 1876, strong floods did what Grant's engineers could not: they changed the course of the Mississippi River in front of Vicksburg. The river now flows south of the city. North of the city, the old bend in the river remains visible. A bypass canal, visible along the left edge of the photo, redirects the Yazoo River to now flow past the Hill City. (Chris Mackowski)

▲ The Warren County Courthouse and St. Paul's Catholic Church dominate the Vicksburg skyline, as sketched by Theodore Davis for *Harper's Weekly*. (*Harper's Weekly*)

that crucial period. He had already come to understand the value of Army/Navy cooperation thanks to operations at Forts Henry and Donelson, but the relationship he cultivated with Porter during early 1863 became especially fruitful for both men and the nation. Grant took the lessons in patience he'd learned on the first road to Corinth—when he almost resigned in frustration—and applied them over a four-month span to keep his undeterred eyes on the objective.

He realized that the physical distance between him and his superior, Henry Halleck in Washington, gave him more freedom to act on his own initiative, assuming success would preemptively forgive any disapproval of his actions. He understood how to sift through useful and unhelpful advice from subordinates, making them feel heard and respected even if he did not follow their guidance. He learned political and interpersonal lessons as well, which made him a better commander and prepared him for greater responsibilities to come.

Grant's counterpart, John C. Pemberton, used those same months less productively. One could argue that he lost site of the forest through the cypress trees that increased in density as time progressed. Ironically, the details of command played to one of Pemberton's strengths (his competency as an administrator), but tackling the myriad of administrative issues distracted him from the on-the-ground military situation. His lack of situational awareness undercut another of his strengths: his expertise as an artillerist. If Pemberton had spent more time in Vicksburg rather than headquartering for much of the time in Jackson, he might have paid more attention to the river defenses. Pemberton's command style inflicted defeat by a thousand cuts, bit by bit, piece by piece, until he was finally overwhelmed and helpless. The loss of the Mississippi River and capture of his army was nothing less than catastrophic.

But first, the Hill City awaited. President Lincoln saw Vicksburg as the key, and Grant, finally on the east bank of the Mississippi River below the bastion, intended to put that key into his pocket.

Bibliography

Bastian, David F. *Grant's Canal: The Unions Attempt to Bypass Vicksburg*. Shippensburg, PA: Burd Street Press, 1995.

Bearss, Edwin C. *The Campaign for Vicksburg Vol. I: Vicksburg is the Key.* El Dorado Hills, CA: Savas Beatie, 2021.

Bearss, Edwin C. *The Campaign for Vicksburg Vol. II: Grant Strikes a Fatal Blow*. El Dorado Hills, CA: Savas Beatie, 2021.

Cadwallader, Sylvanus. *Three Years with Grant*. Lincoln, NE: University of Nebraska Press, 1955.

Farragut, Loyall. *The Life and Letters of Admiral David Glasgow Farragut*. New York: D. Appleton and Company, 1879.

Grant, Julia. *The Personal Memoirs of Julia Dent Grant (Mrs. Ulysses S. Grant).* John Y. Simon, ed. Carbondale, IL: Southern Illinois University Press, 1988.

Grant, Ulysses S. *The Personal Memoirs of Ulysses S. Grant*, Vol. I. Hartford, CT: Charles L. Webster & Co., 1885.

Livermore, Thomas L. *Numbers and Losses in the Civil War*. Boston and New York: Houghton, Mifflin and Co., 1901.

Mackowski, Chris. *The Vicksburg Campaign, 1863: The Inland Battles, Siege and Surrender*. Barnsley, UK: Casemate Publishers in conjunction with Savas Beatie, 2025.

Miller, Donald. *Vicksburg: Grant's Campaign that Broke the Confederacy*. New York: Simon and Schuster, 2019.

Pemberton, John C. *Pemberton, Defender of Vicksburg*. Chapel Hill, NC: University of North Carolina Press, 1969.

Porter, David Dixon. *Incidents and Anecdotes of the Civil War*. New York: D. Appleton & Company, 1886.

Shea, William L., and Terrence J. Winschel. *Vicksburg is the Key: The Struggle for the Mississippi River*. Lincoln, NE: University of Nebraska Press, 2003.

Sherman, William T. *Memoirs of General William T. Sherman*. New York: D. Appleton & Company, 1876.

Simpson, Brooks D., and Jean V. Berlin, eds. *Sherman's Civil War: Selected Correspondence of William T. Sherman, 1860–1865*. Chapel Hill, NC: University of North Carolina Press, 1995.

Smith, Timothy B. *Bayou Battles for Vicksburg: The Swamp and River Expeditions, January 1–April 30, 1863*. Lawrence, KS: University of Kansas Press, 2023.

Smith, Timothy B. *Early Struggles for Vicksburg: The Mississippi Central Campaign and Chickasaw Bayou, October 25–December 31, 1862*. Lawrence, KS: University of Kansas Press, 2022.

Smith, Timothy B. *The Real Horse Soldiers: Benjamin Grierson's Epic 1863 Civil War Raid Through Mississippi*. El Dorado Hills, CA: Savas Beatie, 2018.

Wilson, James H. *Under the Old Flag: Recollections in the war for the Union, the Spanish war, the Boxer rebellion*, Vol. I. New York: D. Appleton & Company, 1912.

Index